A LIFE, WELL...
LIVED!

A LIFE, WELL...
LIVED!

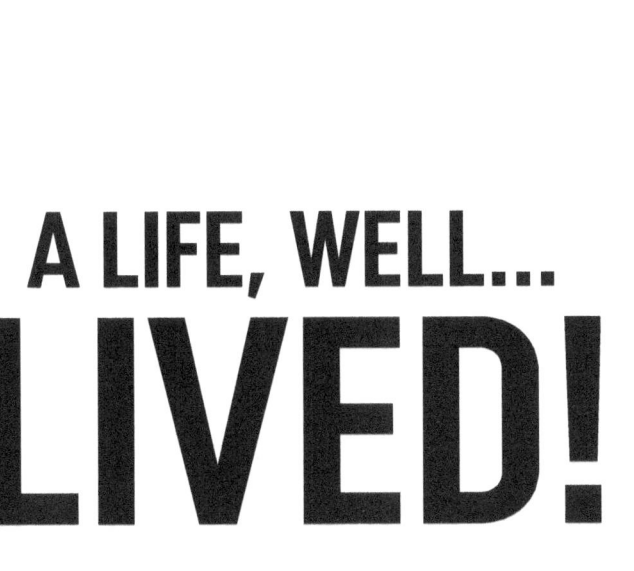

J T FISHER

CITI OF
BOOKS

CITIOFBOOKS, INC.
3736 Eubank NE Suite A1
Albuquerque, NM 87111-3579
www.citiofbooks.com
Hotline: 1 (877) 389-2759
Fax: 1 (505) 930-7244

Ordering Information:
Quantity sales. Special discounts are available on quantity purchases by corporations, associations, and others. For details, contact the publisher at the address above.

Printed in the United States of America.

| ISBN-13: | Softcover | 978-1-959682-86-8 |
| | eBook | 978-1-959682-87-5 |

Library of Congress Control Number: 2023901385

CONTENTS

DEDICATION

To my husband, Milton,
who loved me through my growing pains
to become the woman I am today, and who loves me, still.

To Ruthann L. Ward,
who encouraged me to write again,
and who constantly encourages me to be me.

The events in our lives happen in a sequence in time, but in their significance to ourselves they find their own order.

~~~EUDORA WELTY

PART 1

CHAPTER 1

"So, is this okay with you?" Dana asked the question cautiously. She wasn't sure she wanted to know the answer. Ever so slightly, she started to withdraw her fingers from the side of Michelle's breasts, because she hadn't gotten an answer. She always gave her a back massage after practice. Michelle was an athlete and was always complaining that her back was tight. This time, though, Dana sensed something different. This time, it felt like an invitation to do more than knead the knots from Michelle's shoulders and run her thumbs up and down her spine.

"Yeah, I guess so."

Michelle was tentative at first, too. But then she lifted her torso just a little, allowing Dana's hands to slide under and *caress her more.* Fully cupping the breasts from either side, Dana shifted her straddled position slightly lower so that she was sitting at the base of Michelle's buttocks, and pressing herself against them. Her heart was thumping in her rib cage. It was the same feeling she used to get right before she was to go on stage—exhilaration and fear, excitement and anxiety, all rolled into one.

Michelle let out a soft purr, turning over onto her back toward the wall, which upended Dana, and losing her balance, she fell down gently on top of her roommate. Face-to-face, without a word, they kissed—falteringly at first, but then full on, and passionately.

Dana stopped cold. "What are we doing?" Her voice was raspy.

She cleared her throat. "Are you okay with this?"

Michelle didn't say a word. She got up, took Dana's hand gently, and led her from the common room to the bedroom, locked the door, and then took her in her arms. "Yes, I am." She looked directly into Dana's eyes. "I'm very okay with this."

Michelle was new to making love to a woman but seemed very comfortable with running her hands all over Dana's body, starting with her face and neck. As they stood, fully clothed, in the middle of the bedroom of their dorm suite, Michelle took Dana's cheeks in her hands and brought her face to hers, lightly kissing her forehead, before leading her to bed.

Dana woke up with a start. She was late. She was always late for her nine o'clock class. And she was alone in the room. Michelle was already gone. She was naked. And confused. And panicked. She jumped up out of bed and threw on the nearest pair of jeans, a bra, and a T-shirt, grabbed her backpack, and was out the door in less than five minutes. She didn't even go down the hall to pee or brush her teeth. She would just go during class. *Everyone goes in and out of Dr. Richardson's class. She's so boring.*

Dana tripped down the stairs and out the front door of Monroe Hall, fumbling for the keys to her bicycle lock. Her leg muscles weren't awake yet, so she couldn't get up much speed, but when she reached the top of the hill on University Road, she knew at least she could coast the rest of the way. And there she was. Michelle was coming out of the Kirkland Building. Dana grabbed her brakes and squeezed as hard as she could, almost flipping over the front of her bike.

"Michelle!" she screamed, but couldn't get her roommate's attention. "Michelle, I need to talk." Dana caught up to Michelle, out of breath, out of time, and out of her mind.

"No commitments, okay?" she said, quickly. "What happened last night was a one-time deal, okay?"

She knew this was a lie. She knew she loved Michelle. She had never felt this way about any of her other friends before. This was something strange and exciting, yet she was terrified by it. "I can't do this." She felt a throbbing in her neck.

Michelle just stood there listening. She didn't react in any way to what Dana was saying. Her athletic frame maintained a strong posture, her semi-smile was unscathed, and her arms didn't move from the grasp that she had around her books. Michelle was not the most animated person Dana knew. In fact, it had always been difficult to read her.

Finally, Michelle spoke. "Whatever you want, Dana. I just want you to be happy."

Dana let out a breath of relief. She had no idea what to expect from this particular encounter. She picked up the handlebars and put her right foot on the pedal. She could always get a faster start because for some reason, her right leg was stronger.

"We can talk later tonight." The lump in her throat was noticeable as she choked on the words. She pushed off and went to class, leaving Michelle standing on the street. Michelle knew Dana was lying too, but stood there and watched her ride off.

Dana couldn't concentrate in class. She tapped her pen on the desk for the entire hour, trying to figure out how she felt. She loved Michelle. As a friend. She was *not* a lesbian. She even doodled a little to that effect. "*I am not,*" she wrote. There were no notes taken that hour. She had no idea at all what Dr. Richardson was even talking about. *I'll have to ask someone for notes,* she thought. She didn't care. She had to figure out what to do to get this crap out of her head.

The day seemed to last forever. To top it off, Michelle had practice until six o'clock, so she wouldn't even be home for another two hours. Dana threw some chicken in a pan and aimlessly began to shake some spices on top. She was so distracted that she didn't even realize what she was putting in the pan, so they were going to dine on cinnamon chicken that night.

When Michelle finally walked in the door and threw her backpack on the bed, Dana was down the hall in the community kitchen. Michelle grabbed her stuff for the shower and disappeared down the hall to the girls' bathroom. The girls' dorm bathroom was not her idea of the idyllic place to shower, as she was a bit shy. However, it did trump the locker room at the gym. As she turned the corner and reached for the door, she caught Dana's eye coming down the hall with the pan of chicken.

"I'll just be five minutes," said Michelle. She slipped in behind the bathroom door, barely hearing the response.

"No rush. I haven't made the salad yet."

Dana tried to be cool and calm, but she felt a twinge of excitement in her stomach. At first, she thought she was just hungry. But as the seconds ticked by, waiting for Michelle, she felt a kind of warmth and anticipation growing. The twinge and twitching had intensified, and she felt that familiar warmth between her legs. Trying to convince herself that nothing was going to happen, she knew in her heart that she wanted it. She wanted to be close, feel safe and warm and loved. That's what Michelle offered her. She felt neither pressured nor threatened. She tried to tell herself she didn't need to have a lesbian relationship to get that from her. It didn't have to lead to sex.

Dana pulled the lettuce and some other vegetables out of the refrigerator and turned to put them on the table. Michelle had come in from the hallway and was getting some clothes from the dresser. Dana was frozen. She couldn't take her eyes off Michelle, watching every move she made, in anticipation of her dropping her towel to get dressed. When she did, Dana's heart jumped, and she felt a sudden tingling. That was it. She was convinced she was a lesbian.

Dana turned and tried to concentrate on the salad. Never had carrots and celery been diced so tiny for a salad before. It was then that she realized what she had done to the chicken dish. If Michelle was in the same place in her thinking, then maybe she wouldn't notice. When she finally came into the common room, they sat and ate in silence.

"Take me to the infirmary," Dana gasped. "I can't breathe. Please stop this stuff in my mind." The girls had done a little partying with some of the other people on the dorm floor last night. Smoked a little dope. Nobody else was having problems, but Dana was freaking out. Maybe there was something in the pot. "Please take me to the hospital. I can't catch my breath." Dana pulled at her collar as if she were choking. She was sure she was going to die.

Dana and Michelle waited in the lobby for what seemed like hours. When someone finally called her in to see a doctor, it wasn't even a doctor. It was a nurse who had little patience. Was that it? Was that all they were going to do? She was told to keep busy. She was told that it was just some anxiety. She was told it would pass.

It didn't.

She ended up back at the infirmary the next morning, having spent the entire afternoon and night in the same condition. Everyone around her had thrown up their hands in frustration, having no idea what to do or say. She had been left alone in her misery, so at the crack of dawn, as soon as the doors opened, she was registered, sedated, and then admitted.

When she woke up, Dana was in a single room in the school's infirmary, and a slight man with a Russian accent was standing in the doorway. "Are you awake now?"

He was a shrink. He was a fucking psychiatrist. She had gone nuts, she thought to herself. She rolled over, turning her back to him. There was no way she was going to talk to him— certainly not about doing the drugs or drinking or thinking she was a lesbian.

"May I come in?"

"If you must." Dana had always had a flair for the dramatic. She rolled back over and pulled the covers up around her, making a feeble attempt at being gracious. She was not sure what she was covering up, but she felt safer.

"How are you feeling?" He asked that question as if it was the first on the checklist of questions he was supposed to ask. Then he dropped his shoulders and added; "now that was a stupid question. You're probably feeling pretty low … if not physically from the meds they gave you, for other reasons that brought you here in the first place."

Dana liked him. He didn't pull any punches. Got right down to it. She sat up, still gathering the covers around her. She eyed him from head to toe, determining that he wasn't too threatening. "I had a bad experience with some weed, that's all."

"Okay, I'll accept that." He sat down on a chair next to the bed, casually, as if this whole scenario was an ordinary situation. "My name is Dr. Petrov." Casually crossing one leg over the other, he was making small circles with his ankle. Dana was focused on the motion, and somehow soothed. "What I think you experienced was a panic attack … free floating anxiety. I think maybe your defenses were down from smoking the reefer, and your mind got the best of you." He sat back, reached into the pocket of his drab sweater and pulled out a pipe, while still spinning his foot. There was nothing in the pipe. Dana figured it was just a prop to make her feel secure that he was a real psychiatrist … you, know, Freud like.

"Anything in particular on your mind? Extra stress from class?" He paused, ever so slightly, both his questions and his foot action, not really expecting an answer. "Anything?" He asked. Those were more of the questions from the checklist, Dana thought.

"No, not really." She lied. She had gotten pretty good at lying. "Can I go home now? I feel fine ... just a little woozy from the medicine they gave me." She felt a lot woozy; in fact, she liked the feeling. Sleeping it off had been the best medicine. "What was that stuff, anyway?"

"It's a medicine called Atarax. It's used to treat anxiety." Dr. Petrov spoke very slowly. His command of the English language was lacking slightly, so he took extra time to pronounce things carefully lest he get himself into trouble and have to explain what he meant to people who are already having difficulties.

"Well," said Dana, "It works. It really does. Can I get some to take home with me?" This was one of Dana's best games. She always wanted more of anything that made her feel good.

Dr. Petrov put his pipe in his pocket and stood up, straightening out his sweater. He stepped toward the door, but turned on his heels. "I'd like you to stay with us for a day or two to see how you do on this medicine before I send you home." Apparently this wasn't a game for him.

"Your folks know you're here. If you want, you can call them later." He turned back and started walking toward the door. Again, a swivel back. "I'll check in on you later today. Get some rest. And do yourself a favor ... keep your visitors to a minimum; especially any gentleman friends."

Dana laughed out loud. If he only knew. She doesn't have many friends. Her best friends are guys, and the love of her life is a woman. Go figure. She was pretty fucked up. Just give her another one of those little green pills, she thought.

"We're second class citizens," exclaimed Dr. Petrov. "That's why you have to climb three flights of stairs to see me. That's the only place they could find to house the Mental Health Department of the Infirmary." His office was small, but he had enough room on his walls to display not only his diplomas but also an array of photographs of his family and of several National Parks. The pictures were soothing to look at; Dana thought … *the ones of the waterfalls and the mountains … not the ones of his kids.*

"Can you do me a favor, please?" Dana asked the question sarcastically as she slumped down into the most uncomfortable armchair she had ever come across. "Could you call it 'emotional health' department?" She hated labeling herself as mentally ill; and that's what she felt like when she came to see Dr. Petrov. It had taken her two months since her little episode with the pot to finally tell him about Michelle. She didn't think the fact that she loved Michelle made her mentally ill … it just made her feel anxious and squirrely.

"Is it still going on?" He wanted to know. He wasn't judging her. The sad thing was that he didn't have to. She was judging herself, and harshly. Both Dana and Michelle had started dating men and continuing their relationship on the side, because despite the fact that their feelings for each other were honest and deep, neither one of them could deal with the concept of being in love with another woman. Anita Bryant was waging war against people like them. Their families would never understand. At least Dana knew for a fact that her family wouldn't.

CHAPTER 2

"Mom, this guy has been bothering me every time I go to the pool." Dana was putting the finishing touches on a sandwich that was much bigger than she needed. She had put on a few pounds in the year since college, but didn't seem to care. "What do I do if he asks me out?"

"Go!" Dana's mother was worried that Dana would be an 'old maid.' She was from a different generation (weren't all mothers?) and was married when she was 19, and already had two kids by the time she was Dana's age. Marge had been so busy trying to find men for Dana that she had lost sight of some of the values that she had instilled in her in the first place. "You know, Dana, you shouldn't be so smart and so good at sports around the boys. They don't like that."

Dana intentionally dropped the half sandwich she had in her hand. "Duh, I'm such a clod. Um, what should I do now?" Sarcasm didn't befit her. She immediately apologized. "I'm sorry, mom, but if I try to hide who I really am now, then what happens later on. Do I have to play dumb and klutzy my whole life just to get and keep a man?" She got serious. "I don't want to have to sacrifice who I am for anyone. If someone is going to fall in love with me, they have to fall in love with the REAL me." She held back what felt like tears, but she knew it was more than that. She knew deep down that she had no earthly idea who she was. Dana picked up her sandwich and took it into the dining room, sat down with the newspaper, and silently ate her lunch. She was glad it was Friday, although nothing in the weekend section of the newspaper appealed to her.

Dana finally looked up from the paper and Marge was standing over her.

"Fred was a bore, Mom. He took me to a carnival and stood there while I rode the rides, and I played the games. He didn't even eat a corn-dog. For God's sakes, who goes to a carnival and doesn't eat a corndog?" Dana was really fed up with her mother's pushing her to date. It probably had something to do with the fact that she had suspected something was going on between Michelle and her. Or maybe that was just in Dana's head. Of course there was the time she brought Michelle home for Thanksgiving and sometimes it's hard to hide things. It could have been a glance, or a comment. Or it could have been the fact that they were fooling around all night in her bedroom with her grandparents asleep in the next room. *Did Nana and Grandpa hear something? Did they tell mom?*

"I didn't say you had to marry him." Marge defended herself. "I just thought it might be nice to have a night out. It seems like you sit home all the time."

"My life, my choice." Dana thought back to some of the other winners. There was the guy whose mother owned the clothing store. He was just creepy. She went out with him to appease her mother but boy, was he creepy. He spent more time chasing the pigeons off of her balcony than he did talking to her. At one point, Dana thought he was actually trying to communicate with them.

Then there was the guy who sat there over dinner and told her that he felt like they had skipped the first few levels of relationships. It was because he felt so close to her. Funny, Dana couldn't even remember his last name. First few levels? Does that mean straight from dessert into the sack?

Oh, and the old guy who slobbered when he talked. Dana got sick to her stomach just thinking of the prospect of having to kiss him goodnight. So she didn't. And he never called her for another date.

Dana finished her sandwich, put the dish in the sink and waited for her mother's usual response.

"Can't you put that in the dishwasher at least?"

"Bye, Mom."

"Come here often?" The voice startled Dana, as she had almost fallen off to sleep in the same lounge chair she always used by the pool at her apartment complex. She turned toward the voice and it was coming from a fairly nice looking guy, dressed in business casual street clothes, carrying a beat up briefcase. "If you're going to be here awhile, I'll go put on a suit and join you."

"I thought your roommate said you hate the pool."

"Yeah … but I like what I see sitting beside it!" Andy wasn't bashful, that's for sure. He rested his briefcase on the lounge chair next to Dana. He had just come from an all day insurance seminar so he could maintain his licensing.

"Actually, I've had enough. I was going up to shower and go run some errands."

"Phew! I hate the pool. How about a movie and then out for a drink later?" Andy was persistent. He had been watching Dana in her bathing suit from his balcony for two months, now, and finally got up the nerve to ask her out.

"Uh." She was caught off guard. Her mother was in her head. All she could think of was the conversation she had with her about what to do if he asks her out. "Okay, uh." Dana rummaged through her bag for her keys. "What time?"

"Movie's at eight. Meet you by the elevator at seven fifteen." He grabbed his briefcase with authority, as if he had just closed a major deal and he was gone.

"Phew" she said to herself.

Dana thought back to the first time she met Andy. Imagine, she thought, getting picked up in an elevator. At least it wasn't some sleazy bar. Although his line was kind of gross. "Going down?" he asked, with a sinister grin. It took her weeks to figure out why he was smiling that way. She was, after all, a little slow on the uptake. Oral sex! That's what he meant! Nope.

She didn't want to look too dressy and she didn't want to look too casual. She went through four outfits until she settled on a pair of black jeans and a printed top. What was she thinking? He'd seen her in her bathing suit. He knows how heavy she is. And he's still interested? He must be desperate to get some. Not from me, she thought. Not tonight. Seven fifteen came all too quick.

Andy was wearing white jeans, a red, short-sleeved button down shirt with white buttons, black socks, black loafers, and a black belt. He reminded Dana of someone she had seen on TV, but she couldn't remember who. It wasn't somebody really famous, or really handsome, or really rich. *Damn*, she thought.

"What are we seeing?" she asked. She prayed it wasn't some love story or an action film, and she didn't care much for horror films or science fiction either.

"I'll leave that up to you," Andy offered. "There's a few good ones out there. What kind of movies do you like?"

"I think I could use a laugh." Dana had her fill of movies in college. She took too many film courses and now she couldn't just enjoy a movie for the movie's sake. Besides the fact that she was working for her father in his studio, making local commercials, PSA's and trying to branch out into serial television, she found herself picking movies apart from several points of view. She was what she referred to as the unwanted movie critic.

Andy rattled off a few titles, but Dana couldn't decide. Once again, she couldn't decide. "You choose."

"Take this Job and Shove It!" Andy decided for both of them. Relieved that he had made the decision, Dana followed Andy into the elevator. Dana was relieved that he had picked a comedy, at least. Dana squirmed through the whole film, finding it only mildly entertaining, that is, when she was able to concentrate. She wondered what he would expect of her later. *He didn't buy her dinner, for God's sake.* From what she could determine, he couldn't afford to buy much. They were at the dollar theater, and they were sharing medium-sized popcorn.

After the movie, Andy opened the door to his car, if you want to call it that, and Dana curled up in the front seat amid the hanging tape deck, the bag of newspapers and a gym bag that obviously hadn't been tended to in a while. It smelled like a locker room. At least he himself was clean.

Andy jumped in. "I know a place right down the street on the boulevard we can go for a quick drink." Dana nodded. That was another thing about which she had her apprehensions. If she has a beer, she'll be ordering something inexpensive, which is sensitive to Andy's wallet, but won't come across as proper. She didn't want to come across as low class. If she orders what she really wants, whiskey, she'll be ordering something more expensive, and will look like a lush. Should she order wine? She always gets a stuffy nose when she drinks wine. *Oh, that's just lovely. I'll be sitting there and my nose will be dripping right into my glass.* She never did understand why she had these long battles in her head, worrying so much about what other people thought rather than just being herself and being okay with that.

"I know this place," Dana perked up as they pulled into the parking lot. "This is owned by a friend of mine's dad. In fact, friends of mine and I helped move the furniture in the day before he opened." Dana wondered if Mr. Kingman would even remember her. She had too much to drink that day, and had gotten sick. At least it was in the ladies room, and only Lisa knew about it. At least, she thought only Lisa knew about it. She hadn't had that much beer to drink since college. Beer was for football games, car-washing and maybe the beach.

Here we go, she thought. Here it comes.

The elevator doors opened part way and then stopped. Andy forced his arm through the opening and pushed, and the panels resumed a very slow process of separating enough to slip through. Dana had been stuck on that same elevator for what seemed an eternity just last month. It had only been twenty minutes, but after that experience, she had developed an overblown fear of elevators. She really hated them, and would often opt for the stairs if it wasn't too far. Dana couldn't decide whether her heart was pounding because of the elevator doors or because of what might happen in front of her own apartment door.

It was both. For all her fears about what Andy might want to do or expect from her though, he walked her to her door, and stopped. "Thanks, Dana. I had a really nice time. You're a funny girl."

Dana wasn't quite sure what he meant by that, since she hadn't told any jokes. She quickly rehashed the evening in her mind. She was often naïve and was trying to figure out if that was a come on.

Andy leaned in and kissed Dana on the cheek, turned around and started down the hall. Without turning around, she heard him say, "Let's do it again soon."

The kiss of death. 'Let's do it again soon.' She had enough dating experience to know that he was going to avoid her like the plague. She forced her key in the door. By the time she got it in and looked up and down the hall, he had already disappeared into his corner apartment, probably laughing with his roommate about what a dud she was.

"At least he wasn't like these guys my mother keeps setting me up with," she explained. Dana rolled over in her bed and reached for her coffee. She loved her peaceful Sunday mornings. Often, she didn't get up and dressed and moving until mid-afternoon. "So when can you come down for a visit?"

Michelle didn't answer right away, which convinced Dana that her suspicions were correct. "Are you seeing someone else?"

Michelle hesitated and then finally answered. "Kind of."

While she knew Michelle couldn't see it, Dana's smirk came across in her voice. "Well, and now here's the burning question …" Michelle let the words slither out. "Okay, it's a he. His name is Kevin."

"I'm glad, Michelle." Dana just said that. She wasn't really sure how she felt. She knew it was over between the two of them, and she did, indeed, mourn that fact. "I only want you to be happy." Those were the same exact words that Michelle had used when this whole thing started four years ago.

"Heard that before," said Michelle, sarcastically. "I need to run.

Talk to you soon."

Dana was pretty sure, now, that whatever it was she had had with Michelle was over. She didn't quite know how to feel. She wasn't sure if she should be relieved because it caused so much anxiety, sad because it was the first time she felt safe loving someone and it was over, or happy for Michelle because she had someone special in her life.

Dana had had her first experience with a girl at the age of 11, with a bunkmate at camp. It was, she thought back, that "experimental" thing that a lot of kids go through. She and

Janie had lain naked in Janie's bed, fiddling until it felt good. That was it. She didn't remember feeling anxious or in love. But instead of arts and crafts projects, this is what Dana brought home from camp that summer. She smiled and took a sip of coffee.

"You really got the creeps from that movie, didn't you?" Dana was testing the waters with Andy. This was the second time during their courtship that Andy let on that he was turned off by homosexuality, if not a homophobe. "You want to know how I feel?" she asked.

"Not sure I do." Andy had begun to figure out that Dana was a lot more liberal in her thinking, and certainly a lot more tolerant than he was of other peoples' differences. He lived in a much more myopic world than she.

"I think any person has the capacity to love any other person to any degree, in any way," Dana started. She wasn't sure if their relationship was strong enough yet to take the shock of her sharing her sexual past with him. She was trying very hard to be what she was supposed to be, by dating men and looking for a husband. She wondered sometimes if she was in denial of the reality of what her relationship with Michelle meant to her.

"I disagree." Andy was pretty sure of himself. "You're either gay or you aren't." He paused. "And I'm not altogether sure how people decide they're gay."

Dana laughed out loud. "People don't decide it. They're born that way. It has to do with hormones, sexual tendencies, environment, and all kinds of stuff." Dana was finding herself defending homosexuality to Andy; at the same time, she was trying to quash the memories and feelings of her own homosexual relationship. She wasn't out trolling for women. She wasn't particularly attracted to women. What happened with Michelle just happened.

"Gay men and lesbians are attracted to the same sex. That's all. They have physical, emotional and sexual attraction to people of the same sex." Dana was watching Andy cringe as she spoke. "And what about people that are aroused by both sexes … I mean, don't you get off on watching two girls do it?"

"I guess." Andy took a deep breath. He was noticeably on edge. He was grasping the steering wheel tightly enough that she could see his knuckles turning white. "Can we change the subject? Do you want to go get something to eat?"

"Did you at least like the movie?" Dana loved it. She loves Julie Andrews and Robert Preston anyway, so 'Victor, Victoria,' despite its theme, had a lot on the plus side for her. Besides, it was as funny as hell.

"I guess." Andy didn't really mean it. He just didn't want to talk about it anymore. "Let's get some ice cream somewhere."

Dana closed the door behind Andy after she watched him walk down the hall. She was sure now, that she had scared him off. After all of those cheap dates where they didn't spend any money, like playing racquetball or going to the Home Show with complimentary tickets, Andy had actually spent some money this time. And still, just a kiss at the door.

Dana leaned back on the inside of her apartment door. It wasn't that she didn't believe she actually had a boyfriend. She did wonder, though, what it was that kept Andy hanging around. She wasn't putting out. She didn't see herself as particularly desirable, or pretty. She was certainly no cover girl. Dana really suffered from low self-esteem and a low sense of self-worth. She knew it then. She knew it as a kid. She never felt like she fit in. She was never popular. *So what did he want? What did he see in her?*

He was supposed to come back the next night for dinner. Dana knew her cooking was one reason he liked her, but that couldn't be all of it.

Dana never understood why the boys she liked would never pay any attention to her, but all the ones who liked her were boys in which she had no interest. She hated to think she was shallow, but she was. Thinking back, she remembered this one nice boy named Joey, who really liked her in high school. He would ride his bike up and down the street in front of her house on the off chance that he might see her. Joey had the worst case of acne that Dana had ever seen. It disgusted her to think that he might want to kiss her, and that she would have to get close to those boils and scabs. It made her wince. And then it made her feel guilty.

Then there was that Mitch guy, who asked her out when she was fifteen. They went to a movie, of his choice, because she certainly wouldn't have decided to see an action movie with all the chase scenes, guns and blood. When it was over, they drove awhile and she didn't recognize where they were. Since she wasn't driving herself yet, and they had just moved to the Atlanta area, she didn't know her way around. Mitch parked the car on a dark and narrow street, in what she thought was still Decatur, in front of what looked like a bar. There was a neon sign in the window, but she couldn't make out what it said.

"I'll wait here," she said as he opened the door for her.

"It's okay. I know the guy. He'll serve us." Mitch was confident and almost bragging at the fact that he was only sixteen and could get served liquor.

"Mitch, it's against the law. I don't want to get caught." Dana hadn't budged from the passenger seat of the car. She could feel her heart pounding in her neck.

"You won't. I told ya. I know the guy." Mitch reached in to take her hand.

"Still." she said. "I'll wait here." Dana pulled the door shut. It wasn't as cold as it was the night before, but she still felt a chill. *And what happens when this jerk comes back out. He has to drive me home after drinking who knows what, and then he's going to want to kiss me or more …* Dana's mind went haywire. She was no longer chilled. She was starting to sweat. She opened the door of the car and stepped out, but looking up and down the street, she didn't feel too safe. Rethinking her plan, she got back in the car and locked the doors. *I'll just panic here. At least it's warm,* she thought.

Mitch came back out after only ten minutes. Dana wondered what and how much he drank so fast. He opened the driver's side door and slid in behind the wheel.

"Okay, off we go." They drove in silence back down to the highway, merged uneventfully into traffic and rode in the right lane all the way to their exit. Dana was praying half for a safe trip home and half that he leave her alone. She was beginning to really hate dating. But this Andy … he seemed different. Was it because she was older? She didn't feel any more confident about men. So much had happened between high school and now … but somehow, Andy wasn't as smothering or as threatening. He seemed kinder, safer.

Dana climbed into bed but found herself having to count sheep and play alphabet games in her head just to keep thoughts of what might happen the next night from dancing around in her head. Sleep never came easy to her. Shutting down her thoughts was not a skill she had mastered. She wished they would run other than horror movies on late night television. It was already two in the morning and she was still staring at the ceiling.

"Just help me get the food put away and I'll shove everything in the dishwasher later." Dana jumped up from the table. They had finished off a bottle of wine and a good part of the Coq Au Vin. "We can have dessert and coffee later."

Andy carried the serving pieces into the kitchen. "Who taught you to cook like this?" He was used to eating take-out from the Italian place down the street, pizza and frozen TV dinners.

"I have recipes from my mom, both of my grandmothers, and my Junior High Home Economics teacher." Dana loved to cook. "Cooking is the one thing I can do where I can get cheap accolades for doing something that's really easy." She stacked the dishes in the sink and looked up. "All you need to do is read and follow instructions, and people like it most of the time." This was one of Dana's open admissions of seeking attention, and she freely admitted it, because it was one of few positive ones. As a kid, she looked for attention in so many negative ways. Malingering, melancholy and tantrums had no place in this relationship. Yet.

Without warning, the lights flickered and then went out. "Not again," moaned Dana. The kitchen was extremely dark. She reached out gingerly and brushed Andy's shoulder. "We have two choices." She fumbled around on the counter for a pack of matches. "The hallway has emergency lights, or we can go sit out on the balcony. It shouldn't be too cold."

"Balcony." Andy's response was immediate. His roommate had company, so he couldn't go home yet, and it was only 9:30. "We can go out there and talk." Andy made note of the fact that Dana didn't offer up her bedroom.

Dana lit a match and the two of them stumbled through the semi-darkness to the sliding glass door that led out to her diminutive balcony. They both knew they were living in a less than glamorous building in an even less desirable neighborhood, but when you are young and just starting out, you do the best that you can. Dana had a limited budget. She was able to make it at least homey and comfortable, having added some hanging plants and a cute little ice cream table with two chairs.

There they sat for three hours, talking and getting to know each other.

And laughing. They did a lot of laughing. Dana was actually surprised at how relaxed she was with Andy. She felt no pressure to perform and she really felt like she could be herself. Her mother's words danced in her head for a short time, but she was able to push them out. *Don't be so smart and so good at sports around the boys." This one likes me for who I am mom, sorry.*

Andy finally stood and stretched. "I better get going. I have to get up early for work tomorrow." He stepped toward the glass door and turned back, his mind half-fixed on a first-time appointment with a new insurance client and the other half fixed on Dana, still stretched across the ice cream chair. "When did the lights go back on? I didn't even notice."

"About an hour ago," Dana scrambled to her feet to follow him in. At the door of her apartment, Andy turned around and quickly kissed Dana on the forehead. "Goodnight," he started. "You know, you're really good company." He smiled, turned on his heels, and he was off, down the hallway.

Dumbfounded, Dana closed the door behind him. She turned around and gently fell back against the door. She was in love.

A movie here, racquetball there. An inexpensive dinner, a picnic in the park. Dana really liked hanging out with Andy. He made her laugh. She was attracted to him, she knew that. While she had what she knew was her own sexual past, she had never been with a man, short of jerking a guy off. So she was scared, too. Although she had no idea what to expect, she had made her mind up to try to let things unfold naturally.

"Let's try this thing." Dana opened the cabinet under her TV set and pulled out her Magnavox computer game as they sat cross-legged on the floor in front of the television. She had chosen this one because it already had a keyboard, and she was convinced that Magnavox would be the first to develop a program to turn the thing into a home based computer. For now, though, it only had a few games on it. She had a few sports games and some word games so far. She even had a stock market game, and although she knew Andy was trying to build a base in the life insurance business, she also knew that he loved to read the stock pages and watch that TV show, *what was it? Oh yeah, Wall Street Week in Review.* She couldn't say the guy's name and she sure as hell couldn't get that stupid theme song out of her head. They watched it every Friday night before they went anywhere or did anything.

"What game do you want to play?" Dana didn't have a preference. She spent hours playing all of them. It was almost as if she was addicted to them. She had pain in her wrists from playing with the Rubik's cube and still hadn't figured it out. She loved games.

"What's this Scramble game?"

"Okay, turn around. I'll put in a word and then push the scramble button. Then you have to try to guess the word by trying one letter at a time. It can be fun if we add some high stakes to it." She paused for a moment. "Let's just try it once first. She typed in the word 'compassionate'. "Okay, turn around."

"Hmmm. S … T … O … Wait, no." Andy hit the start again button. "C … A … M … P …"

"You're close. Try again." She was happy. She had him stumped.

After a few tries, Andy figured out the word. He then put in the word 'quarterback'.

Dana got it on the first try. Her second word was 'available'. The machine did a great job scrambling this one. He'll never get it, she thought. Dana liked winning.

"Hmmmm. A … V … A … I … L Available! Ha! Got it on the first try. Are you trying to tell me something?" Andy looked hopeful. Dana was incensed. "Why is everything always about sex? It was just a word." She sat back against the coffee table. "I could say the same thing about your choice of word. Quarterback? Come on, really."

Dana pulled out the game cartridge and stuffed in another one. This time they were going to play a game that couldn't possibly lead him on. She was almost angry.

"What do you want from me?" Andy was starting to get frustrated. "Compassionate? Available? What was I supposed to think?" "How about, 'gee, she picked words with lots of vowels to try to confuse me?'" Dana was now being sarcastic. Let's just play this stock market game, okay?"

"Andy, not here." Dana pushed him away. "For God's sake, this is my parent's bed." They had been watching television in the back bedroom, because that was the only one that was hooked into this new cable television thing. Dana couldn't get over the kinds of things that she could see on the TV. What baffled her more was the fact that her mother could watch those things, and probably did watch. *Ewww*, she thought to herself.

"So, let's go in the other room." Andy's erection was pressing against his shorts. Dana hated those stretchy knit short shorts guys were wearing. They all thought they were NBA players and what's worse, they all thought girls wanted to see their shit dangling. "Come on, Dana." He was all over her tonight. She knew that sooner or later she would have to give in. She was frozen.

"I don't think this is the time or the place Andy. You're making me feel really uncomfortable."

Andy rolled his eyes back into his head and fell back on Dana's father's pillow. That turned her stomach even more. It wasn't so much that he was frustrated about not getting into her jeans. It was more, she thought, that by doing what he just did, he successfully lodged her father's image into her mind. What a buffoon. He made me like this, she thought. Don't think it was the intended result, but nevertheless, he's the main reason she couldn't be less "frigid."

"Yoo hoo, Dana? Are you there? I'm really okay with this." Andy was trying to be tactful. He wasn't used to girls like Dana. His old girlfriend, he had found out sadly, was a slut. Julie had been sleeping around on him, to get what she wanted, and then dumped him when she realized he wasn't going to be the sugar daddy that she thought he would be. His career wasn't taking off fast enough. There wasn't enough money for her. He didn't want that type of girl either, but he hadn't come across a girl like Dana before ... one who wasn't really interested in sex at all. He didn't think it was him. He hadn't ever really had a problem moving a relationship along to the point where he could at least get something. "When you're ready, okay?"

"It'll have to be." Dana got up and left the room.

"Okay, I'm going to do this." Dana had been talking to herself all afternoon. *This is ridiculous.*

He's not going to wait around for me forever. I have to get overthis. Dana paced back and forth in her apartment. She had taken the afternoon off after her visit to the gynecologist. No point in going back to work for only an hour or so.

She thought back. There was no trouble letting the boys feel her up when she was eleven. Not until they got caught, anyway. Even at that social at camp, when that kid ... Geez, she couldn't even remember his name ... put his arm around her shoulder, and dangling his forearm over, was able to gloss over her nipple with his fingertips. She felt the sensation right through her shirt. It made her stomach tingle a little. If felt good. And when he pulled her closer, he was able to get a better handle, cupping her breast (what little of it there was when she was twelve), while he turned her head to continue the longest make-out session she had ever known. It all ended when the P.A. system announced that the social was over and that the boys had to board the bus. Dana remembered squirming for one last kiss and feeling a slight wetness between her legs. Naiveté was her ally there, and thankfully she didn't ask anyone about it.

She had been the aggressor when it had come to Michelle. But she also freaked out after it happened. She still believes that's why she ended up in the hospital sedated that time. Hasn't smoked dope since, that being the unintended benefit. It didn't stop her from continuing that relationship way too long, she determined.

She barely even pleasures herself anymore. How was she going to do THIS? Andy was a really nice guy. She really cared about him. Was she saying this stuff out loud or was it still just in her thoughts? *'Shit. I'm losing it again.'* Dana turned on the radio. She paused and then turned it back off. Then she opened the door of her apartment and looked up and down the hallways. *Nobody is home this early. It's not like I can even drop in on anyone to hang out,* she thought to herself.

Dana crossed through the living room and out onto her patio. Rush hour was just beginning. Andy wouldn't even be home from work for another hour. She took a deep breath and went into the utility closet, dragging out the ironing board into the middle of the living room. She turned on the television, and then went into the bedroom and dragged out the laundry basket. At least she could do something productive while waiting, to take her mind off of it for a little while.

She tuned into the Phil Donohue Show and proceeded to begin working on her least favorite household chore. Lost in the inane conversation, Dana managed to iron three blouses and a pair of trousers before there was a knock at the door.

"Hold on a minute." She quickly turned off the iron and stripped down to just her underpants, tossing her clothes out of sight, on the armchair.

"Hey – you okay?" Andy knocked again.

Dana tossed a small tablecloth over the ironing board and picked up the iron. "It's open."

Andy opened the door slowly. When he realized what was in front of him he quickly closed it behind him, and locked it, complete with chain lock. He dropped his briefcase and started over to Dana, reaching up at his neck trying desperately to rip apart the perfect Windsor knot he had tied in the tie that morning. The perfect Windsor knot. That was important to him. "Crap." He couldn't get it off fast enough.

Dana kept ironing, trying very hard not to make eye contact, but she couldn't help but laugh at him. He was always so fucking particular about his tie. She wondered how he felt about the perfect knot now.

"What's so funny?" By now, not only did Andy pull his tie and shirt over his head, but his pants and underwear were also gone, and he stood in front of the ironing board with a rock hard erection, still wearing his black socks.

"You."

"Well it's not every day that I walk into your apartment to find you ironing."

Dana smiled, and silently stepped out from behind the ironing board, took Andy's hand and led him to the bedroom.

CHAPTER 3

"So do I renew my lease or not? I mean, they want to tack on an extra $15.00 a month if I don't sign another year lease. I can stay month-to-month, but my budget is tight. Fifteen bucks is a lot of money." Dana sat on the edge of the twin bed in her bedroom. Andy rolled over, reached for his glasses on the nightstand and fell back into the pillow.

"I don't know what to tell you." He knew what he wanted to say, but he wasn't ready.

"All right, I'll go month to month." Dana was resigned to the fact that this guy couldn't make a commitment. "But just imagine waking up like this every morning." She paused. "Hopefully with a little bigger bed …" She stood up, leaned over Andy, allowing her robe to open, and kissed him on the forehead.

As she tried to stand up, he pulled closer and buried his face between her breasts. "Mmmmm, you smell good." He tried to pull her even closer, but she resisted.

"Come on, I'm dripping wet from the shower. I have to get ready for work." Dana spun around, allowing her robe to drop to the floor, knowing full well that Andy's eyes were fixated on her. She began to hum softly under her breath. She knew just the right song to get her message across. "Our house ... is a very, very, very fine house ..." Her voice trailed off as she disappeared into the closet.

Andy threw the cover off, and sat up on the edge of the bed, rubbing his eyes. He glanced over his right shoulder at his reflection in the mirror, and thought to himself, '*why would she want to wake up looking at this every morning.*' His hair was disheveled; his face was puffy to the point where he could barely open his eyes. By the time he had pulled himself together enough to stand up, Dana bounced out of the closet fully dressed.

"I have a meeting at the studio early, and then I have to be downtown to pitch some two-bit law firm for an ad." She hated driving to downtown Atlanta. She knew she would get caught in rush hour traffic coming back up. She never understood why things got so bottled up so early in this god-forsaken city. "Wish we could do most of our work out here. I'll be back sometime between six and eight depending on 285." Dana really wanted this account. A 30-second television ad for this prestigious law firm, even if it was just a local ad, would be a great move away from those cheap ambulance chasers with whom they had been doing business. She really wanted to start to elevate their reputation.

Andy almost opened his mouth. He was paralyzed. He couldn't do anything but say, "Have a good day."

She was gone.

"So, Andy, what should I do about my lease?" Dana, once again, sat on the edge of the twin bed in her bedroom. Andy rolled over, and again reached for his glasses. This scenario seemed all too familiar to him.

"I don't know what to tell you. We're stuck in our lease until May, and James and I aren't planning on staying here anyway. Getting kind of seedy, if you know what I mean." Dana rolled her eyes. Sometimes he's so dense, she thought. She didn't give a shit about what James was planning. James was nothing but a fly in her ointment. Besides, James had already shown her his opinion of women. Apparently, she wasn't fit to be a corporate wife. At least, that's what he had told Andy early on in their courtship. Dana didn't particularly have a lot of respect for him. It was like James was still living in the 60's or something. *Putz*, she thought.

"Want some coffee? I have a few minutes before I have to go, and the pot is almost finished perking." She laughed to herself as she flitted towards the kitchen. She still had her old drip pot from college and was actually still using it up until about two weeks ago, when she used her S & H green stamps to finally join the 80's and get herself an electric coffee pot.

"Sure, thanks." Andy sat up in bed and started rifling through the *Constitution*. He had heard something about a merger with the Journal. His only interest right now was the odds for Sunday's Falcon's game. He wasn't doing too well in the office pool and wanted to at least know the spread before he went into work. He could read the rest of the paper at lunch.

"You see … You could have this kind of pampering every morning." Dana set the coffee down on the nightstand. "Think about it while I'm in the shower!" She disappeared in to the bathroom.

What Dana didn't know was that Andy thought about it all the time. He just didn't know what to do about it. Was he really ready to get married? Was his financial future secure enough to take on the responsibility of a wife, and later a family? He needed to build his business up to have regular residual income, in case he had a bad month here and there. And, the big question … Is he in love with her? Or just in love with the idea of love? Does he want to, as Dana's grandfather suggested, buy the cow if he's getting the milk for free? He laughed out loud. *Her grandfather. What a sketch.*

"What's so funny?"

"Nothing. Just thinking about something your grandfather said to me the other night." Andy got up, grabbed one more sip of coffee, and moved toward the bathroom while he disrobed. "Can I join you?" "Nope! I'm done." Dana was stepping out of the shower and already had a towel around her glistening body. "No time this morning. Gotta run." She breezed by him. "So should I sign a lease or go month-to-month?"

"The hell with the lease." Andy stood there, butt-naked. "Marry me."

Dana burst into laughter. "That had to be the most pathetic marriage proposal ever."

"Good job, Dana. Way to emasculate me."

"I'm sorry. I didn't mean to laugh. But look at you."

Andy looked down and realized that she was right. He was standing in the middle of the bathroom, wearing nothing, shivering from the chill of the morning air, and had just asked the love of his life to marry him by saying "to hell with the lease …"

"That's why I love you, Andy." Dana put her arms around him and kissed him full on.

CHAPTER 4

"Stop squirming, I can't get the eye-liner on." Liz was getting frustrated with Dana. Ever since she met her, she had never seen Dana wear make-up. Not for anything, not even a date. But here it was her wedding day, and Liz was going to see to it that Dana was the most beautiful bride ever.

"I hate that shit. It makes my eyes itch." Dana really did hate make-up. Her mother was always nagging her to put on a little lipstick. She hated lipstick. *It makes me look like a whore,* she thought.Liz leaned back on the bed.

"Okay, let's take a break." She was sitting on the very bed in which Dana and Andy would later consummate their marriage, although she knew they were already 'doing it.' Liz was the only one who Dana talked to about her sex life, and then only her heterosexual one. "Oh Jesus, look at this." Liz slid her hand to the side on the bedspread, and pointed to where the words FUCK BED were clearly scrawled. "Guess this really is the honeymoon suite. Eww."

"Come on," Dana said. "Let's get this over with." Liz was Dana's best friend. Had been since freshman year. Dana doesn't even remember what brought them together other than the fact that Liz had walked into Dana's dorm room while she was playing her guitar, sat down on the bed and started singing. They had been inseparable ever since except when Liz left for Medical School. They had often talked about doing that together, but Dana, once again, didn't think it was something she would be able to do, or do well, so she didn't try.

The two girls squeezed into the bathroom just as Dana's mother, Marge, burst in the room. "Are you decent?" She had an entourage of men behind her, none of whom Dana recognized.

"Wait!" They both slipped robes on over their undergarments, as they had been trying to cool off in just their bras and slips.

"There is no air conditioning on the first floor, so I told them to bring all the bridal party flowers up here for the time being." Marge went directly over to the thermostat and tapped it down another five degrees.

"How are you girls doing?" Marge spun around. She was, Dana thought, glowing. Her mom was so happy that we had reached this day, and she really liked Andy. Dana wasn't too sure Dad was on board yet, but Mom was definitely happy.

Dana lit up another cigarette. "Fine, mom."

"Oh, Dana! Lipstick! I'm so happy." She was gone.

"I'll be right back." Liz got up to close the door behind her, and then slipped back into the bathroom.

Dana took a long draw on her cigarette. Glad she's happy. Dana had promised herself she would stop smoking after this day was over. She pondered whether she was doing this for herself or for her mother.

She had allowed her mother to make all of the plans for this wedding. Marge hadn't been able to be a part of the planning for the boys' weddings, so Dana had told her, "As long as I don't absolutely hate it, you can do whatever you want." Dana's parents had offered cash or a wedding to Andy and Dana, but they opted for the wedding. Another choice made for other people. Dana hadn't ever 'dreamed' of a wedding day. She had never been the type to flip through bridal magazines. She even hated the game, 'Mystery Date.' She was definitely not a girly girl.

Dana loved Andy. There was no question about that. She anticipated a decent future with him. He had drive and ambition; he had a great sense of humor; he was good looking (she liked him better in jeans and a tee shirt rather than the stuffy suits he wore to work); and most importantly, she didn't have to hide the fact that she was intelligent, athletic and capable from him. He did have a tendency to be a little stubborn about some things. The only thing she worried about is what her mother-in-law-to-be had said to her on the sly. She warned her that Andy can be very selfish. Dana laughed out loud.

"What's so funny?" Liz had emerged from the bathroom fully dressed and completely made-up. She looked fabulous. Ever since college, Dana had clung to her friend Liz. They had been through a lot together, having both gotten the same degrees, they had taken a lot of classes together. They lived across from each other on the same dorm floor for two years, and had a lot in common. Liz, though, had lost her father during her sophomore year, and Dana was there to support her, but she didn't really know what to do or say, since she had such negative feelings about her own father.

But here she was, her friend Liz, the doctor. Dana had told everyone it was because she was burned out from school, that she didn't pursue a graduate degree or follow through on their pact but in her heart she knew that if someone like Liz was going to become a doctor, then she had no business even trying. Liz was so full of confidence. She was so smart.

"Wow!" Dana stood up. "Nobody is going to be looking at the bride." She walked over to Liz and fluffed the ruffle on her right shoulder. "I was just thinking about how many girls I know that go into relationships thinking they're going to change the men they're with." Dana spun around and stepped toward the closet. "Andy will be one of the men who never changes," she continued as she pulled her bridal gown off of its hanger. "He better get used to eating his steak a little more well-done, though."

"Help me into this thing." Dana dropped her robe and started to step into the gown. "I haven't even tried this thing on since the day I bought it. Hope I didn't gain any weight." She lifted her left foot and stepped in, but lost her balance falling back down onto the bed. "Well, that will make it easier." She pulled the dress toward her as she slipped her right leg in, finding then the floor with her feet, she stood up.

Liz got behind her and helped her pull the dress up over her hips as she glided her arms through the cap sleeves. Ugh, so much lace. She thought back to the day she had shopped for it with her mother. She had only tried on three dresses, none for which she had taken off her blue jeans and sneakers. She had even asked the bridal consultant if they made Adidas in slipper satin. She bought the first one she tried on. Marge and Dana took care of the dress, the flowers, the photographer, the band and more than half of the trousseau in one day.

After Liz got the zipper up to the top, she began buttoning. The satin covered buttons were a pain, but they definitely made the dress. The tiny pearl and lace insets on the front were stunning, in lieu of a plunging neck-line. Dana didn't want anything showing to anyone, so the dress was very modest, and only slightly ornate. It was so typical of her taste: understated elegance. It was going to be a beautiful night.

Marge burst in again. "It is so freaking hot down there. They are moving the reception to a different floor. We're still going to do the wedding in the atrium, and then the cocktail party where we originally planned, but then everyone is going to have to go upstairs to the patio ballroom for the dinner." She was so busy talking about the details, Marge didn't notice her daughter. When she finished fiddling with the flowers, she looked up.

Marge put her hands to her chest. For the first time in her adult life, she was speechless. Her eyes reddened, and filled. "Oh, my baby. My little girl, you look exquisite."

"Thank you, Mom." Dana smiled. She felt like she had given her mom a fabulous gift, like the ice skates she had gotten when she was twelve. "When do we go down?"

"In about ten minutes. Almost everyone is here." Marge grabbed a tissue from the box next to the bed and dabbed at the corners of her eyes. "Did I smear my make-up?"

"You look magnificent, Mom." She looked at her mother differently for the first time in a long time. They had gotten past so many years being contrary with each other. She had finally realized that her mom was really only out for her best interests, and loved her very much. And her mother was so beautiful. "Have you seen Andy?"

"Andy is down there having a good time with friends and family. He does look a little nervous, but he's fine." Marge neglected to mention that he was a little pasty from too much drinking the night before.

Dana sat down on the edge of the bed and lit another cigarette. "Really, Dana? In your wedding dress? What if you burn a hole in it?" Marge hated the fact that Dana was still smoking, after all they had come out with against it.

"I'll be careful."

"Liz, can you help me carry the bridal party bouquets downstairs? I have to get the boutonnieres pinned on the boys before we get this shindig started." *Shindig*? Dana thought. *My mother is so strange.* "Sure." Liz picked up the box of boutonnieres and two of the bridesmaids bouquets. Marge got the other three bouquets and the mother and father of the bride and groom corsages and boutonnieres. "Do I need to call you or will you just come down in five minutes?" Marge asked Dana. "You're not going to bolt, are you?"

"I'm fine, mom. I'll be down in five minutes and wait by the side room, just like the caterer told me to." Marge and Liz left her there for the last five minutes of her single life. She turned on the television and watched some college football.

There had been a nine month courtship, a nine month engagement and now here she was. Dana had taken the path of least resistance. She loved Andy. She knew that in her heart. And the sex was pretty good, although she really didn't have much to compare it to, with a man, that is. She knew she had a lot to learn.

There she stood, waiting for the huge bridal party to make their way down that long aisle. It seemed like it was taking forever. Her mind was lost in the song she had so carefully selected to use for the processional. Her father was practically holding her up with his arm under her right elbow, and her mom was all grins, with her arm gently wrapped around her left arm. Well, she was doing exactly what was expected of her. She was marrying a nice boy, about to start her life just the way she was supposed to. Then they would expect a family. Now everyone will be happy.

She kept trying to convince herself this was right. In her heart, Dana knew there was something else that lived within her that she would have to squash, or at least come to terms with. She was pretty sure she had gay or at least bi-sexual tendencies. She knew she was afraid of men, a little, and for sure, afraid of sex. For God's sakes, she hadn't really had sex with Andy without at least little sauce in her. Her mind wandered back to the very first time she gave in to him.

It was only after she had consulted her gynecologist. *What a wimp*, she thought to herself. She had to ask a doctor what to do. She had been there for a regular annual visit, and was sitting in the chair opposite the doctor. She liked this guy. She had been going to him since her sixteenth birthday, when he treated her for those fucking cramps she got every month. He loved the fudge she made, and he always had a drawer full of chocolate. Anyone who loves chocolate that much is okay in her book.

"So, Doc," she started. When is the last time, during this sexual revolution, have you had a 24 year old woman sit across from you, who's still a virgin?" She thought approaching the conversation with humor would make it easier for her, and maybe he would give her some relaxed answers.

"Last week," he sat back in his chair, yet answered quickly, "but then, she was a nun." He opened the famous drawer, reached in and pulled out a Hershey Bar, tossing it across the desk at Dana. "Talk to me."

"Well, I happen to have the most patient boyfriend," she said, wiggling in her chair. "I've been seeing him about four months, but I seem to be a little paralyzed when it comes to letting down and having relations with him." She took a deep breath. She didn't want to get into details about her fear, her distaste and her sexual past. "I really don't know what's stopping me. I mean, I do, but it's not something I can talk about easily." She was stilted. "We've kind of been fiddling around, but no intercourse."

"Jesus Dana," he said. "If you care about him, and you want the relationship to flourish, go with the flow naturally." He took a big bite of his chocolate bar. This guy wasn't really known for his bedside manner. "Go home, get naked, and tell him 'Fuck me, now!'"

Dana thought he was kidding. Her jaw dropped. She couldn't imagine being bold enough to do something like that. "Really?"

"You have to just get over the hump." He waited for a reaction, and got none. The doctor took another bite of chocolate. "Look, sex is normal animal behavior. It's not dirty, it's not perverse. It is simply another way to build intimacy in your relationship. Just go home and show this guy that you care about him. There are," he added, "the times when it's just plain sex for sex's sake."

That was the first time Dana made the connection that men identified sex with love. She was still full of fear, because she assumed it would open up a floodgate. If she had sex with Andy, then she would always have to do it. She did care about him, but could she really do this?

"Thanks doc. I'll give it my best shot." She got up slowly, feeling as though she didn't really get the answers she needed, but reached for the chocolate bar on the desk anyway, and put it in her purse. "See you next year."

Dana went home, and obsessed about it all afternoon. She tried to distract herself by ironing, but eventually did what she was told. The ironing board became her ruse.

"Dana, let's go." Marge had to jerk Dana gently by the arm, to bring her back to the present. "Hold your head up high. You make the most beautiful bride. I'm so proud of you." Dana put one foot slowly in front of the other, keeping her eyes straight ahead, on Andy, to whom she was about to promise the rest of her life.

"If a picture paints a thousand words ..." The music played evenly and Andy took Dana in his arms. They had actually practiced this a few times, because while Andy looked quite debonair in his tuxedo, he had absolutely no rhythm. Dana had picked this song to be "their" song, even though Andy claims he didn't really know any Bread songs. Dana would have picked a song from the forties or fifties because she just loved those old standards, but that would have been even harder for Andy to understand. He just didn't get music. The two of them had taken the trouble to learn a few dance steps on the patio of her parents' home during the weeks prior to the wedding. Dana was looking forward to watching her parents on the dance floor, because the one time Marge and Ben were really in tune with each other was when they were in each other's arms and Glenn Miller was playing.

Dana was all smiles on the dance floor, though the song really had no beat to it. The words were just perfect. *"If a man could be two places at one time I'd be with you, tomorrow and today, beside you all the way ..."* She just loved that. Everyone was watching. She wondered if they could tell that she was leading.

The reception was everything her mother had wanted it to be. Marge was in her glory, jumping from table to table, visiting everyone and chatting with them. She had insisted on a band. "It has to be at least a five-piece combo, with a great vocalist," she had said. "And we have to keep your father away from the stage, except for his toast." The prime rib was perfect, the flowers divine, and Dana even carried the wedding bouquet that Marge had picked out. It had the same kinds of flowers that she had carried twenty-seven years prior. The room was full of industry people, cousins, aunts and uncles, and just a few of Dana and Andy's friends.

Ben held up a glass of champagne in his left hand, and with the microphone in his right hand, commanded the attention of his 180 guests. "Excuse me," he started. The clatter of salad forks and the hum of the chatter continued. "Hello?" The waiters stood still with champagne trays in hand.

The band helped Ben out with a drum roll. A loud one. "Thank you." Ben acknowledged the assistance of the drummer and continued. "Thank you everyone, for being here today to share this special day with us. Our daughter begins a new path today, on the arm of a very nice young man. If you do anything to hurt her, I'll break that arm." Ben was expecting at least a little laugh, but the guests simply murmured. Most of them were used to Ben's dry sense of humor.

"May they have a happy and long life, together. May their stumbles be few, and their triumphs, great. Here's to Dana and Andy! Please welcome Andy's best man, James."

James took the microphone and Dana tried not to cringe, at least not visibly. She didn't know what to expect. Ever since Andy told him about the engagement and asked James to be the best man, James had been threatening to embarrass her with this toast.

"Good evening. I have been Andy's roommate for the past four years, through college and through Andy's courtship of, and engagement to Dana. I imagine there are things that Dana will be able to give him that I haven't. I know she's a better cook than I am." He paused, expecting a laugh. "You'll have to use your imagination about anything else, folks." It was then that the guests snickered.

"I do know, though, that Dana will be getting a great guy, who, if they can get over their differences about who went to the better University, will be a wonderful life mate! Here's to Dana and Andy!" "Here's to Dana and Andy," the crowd echoed. The band kicked in immediately with a medley of songs from the Supremes. People jumped up to dance, and servers began to whirl around the room with trays of Prime Rib. That was another one of the things that Marge had insisted upon. She was not going to serve rubber chicken at her only daughter's wedding.

At some point after the garter was taken off, the bridal bouquet had been tossed and various other traditional wedding rituals had been completed, Dana and Andy disappeared out the back door of the ballroom, and stole away to their honeymoon suite. They had intended to come back down in their travel clothes. That was the plan they had made with Marge. In fact, Dana and Marge spent days looking for just the right outfit for her to wear to leave on her honeymoon. When they got upstairs, Andy ripped off his bowtie, slipped off his jacket and began the tedious affair of unbuttoning those damn satin buttons on the back of Dana's dress.

Within three minutes, they were down to their underwear, and had immediately started rifling through the envelopes, counting the money that would help them begin to build their lives, or at least pay for the trip. They never did make it back down to the reception.

CHAPTER 5

Dana and Andy held on to the door handles for dear life. The taxi driver lived up to the reputation that San Francisco cab drivers had. He barreled down the hills hitting bumps and pot holes with no regard whatsoever for the comfort and safety of his fares. *There isn't even a damn safety belt to hold me in,* Dana thought. Andy glanced at her and squeezed her hand. He knew she wasn't a big fan of travel to begin with, but this was their honeymoon, and he wanted her to be happy and comfortable. He remembered what his Dad had told him, "Happy wife, happy life."

The cab squealed to a stop in front of the Jack Tar Hotel. The cabbie jumped out and opened the door for Dana. Andy begrudgingly let go of her hand as she slid to the side and climbed out. As he opened the door on the street side, he heard a squeal of tires and the blaring of a horn. Another cab swerved and barely missed the door he had just opened. He lurched back, and as he did, his wallet fell from his hand to the ground. Andy bent over to pick it up. The cabbie was getting impatient, as he had already unloaded the luggage and his wife.

Dana and Andy walked into the lobby of the hotel, luggage in hand and wandered to the front desk. Andy cleared his throat. "Reservation for Andy Gordon, please."

Dana pouted. "Excuse me, but isn't the reservation for Mr. and Mrs. Andy Gordon?"

Noticing Dana's wilted corsage, the clerk broke into a smile. "Happens all the time, ma'am. We have the honeymoon suite waiting for you Mrs. Gordon."

Andy's face turned red. "I wasn't even thinking. I'm sorry honey."

Dana blushed. That was the first time anyone had called her that. It was something she would have to get used to. Apparently, Andy was going to have to get used to it as well.

The valet pushed the button in the elevator and looked upwards, while Andy and Dana, holding hands, gently kissed. He rolled the luggage cart out of the elevator and down an ornate hallway. Andy and Dana were not used to such lavish décor. They hadn't traveled together before, except to go camping, and their tent didn't have crystal chandeliers, nor did it have velvet flocking on the walls.

The valet stopped at room 613, put the key in the door and pushed open, pulling the luggage cart in behind him. He swung the two suitcases from the cart right into the closet, spun around, and asked, "Is there anything else?"

Dana nudged Andy and whispered, "You need to tip him." Andy raised his shoulders, as if to question how much.

Dana rubbed her cheek, extending two fingers. He didn't get the message. He whispered back, "How much?" Dana rolled her eyes. Sometimes he is so dumb. She just held two fingers up this time, and decided that if he didn't understand that message, she was just going to have to get an annulment.

Andy reached in his pocket for his money clip and pulled off two dollars, handed them to the valet and closed the door behind him. By the time he had spun around, Dana had already found a bottle of champagne on ice, a tray of fruit and cookies and a congratulatory note from the management. "I think I'm going to like honeymoons."

Andy added, "Me too. I especially liked the bottle we got on the plane. That flight attendant was funny as hell." Andy thought back to their travels. His roommate had picked them up from the hotel brutally early, but got them to the airport late, having gotten stuck in traffic. Atlanta is impossible at rush hour. When the flight attendant did what they thought was going to be the usual pitch, Andy thought it was really funny. 'The mistletoe hanging at the door wasn't that they had the wrong season … it was just one last chance to kiss your luggage goodbye;' or later in the flight when he had everyone take their socks off, giving a bottle of wine to the one with the biggest hole in the toe. Andy laughed out loud, though, when the flight attendant came back on the loud speaker in mid-flight, telling everyone to look out the plane to the right, and they would see Elvis Schmucker's hog farm.

Dana had elbowed him in the ribs for laughing so hard. She hadn't found too much of it that funny. Sometimes she didn't get his sense of humor, but he was hers, for better or for worse. She was too busy clinging to the armrest every time the plane hit a pocket of turbulence. She hated flying.

"Wanna open this now?" Dana asked Andy.

Andy looked at his watch which was still on Eastern Time, while munching on a cookie, and said "Sure, why not?" It was seven back in Atlanta, but only four in California. It was a little early to go to dinner, even though he was already getting hungry. "Let me have it." He bent down the wires, aimed the bottle at the wall, and positioned his thumbs against the plastic stopper. Andy didn't have a lot of practice with champagne. He preferred bourbon and coke, if he drank anything at all. The stopper blew with a vengeance, careened off the wall, and landed right back in the ice bucket. "That was convenient" he said with satisfaction. "Couldn't do that again if I tried!" It didn't take them long to finish the champagne. Although Dana was irritated by the bubbles, she drank it down as if it were water. Last night, after the wedding, they didn't 'consummate' the marriage. After all, they'd been having plenty of sex all along. She knew, though, that the honeymoon was going to be full of it. She had to make sure she was ready to respond. Andy sipped slowly on his, and reached over to Dana, twirling his finger on first, her arm, and then very soon, her breast. He put his glass down, and then his glasses.

Dana knew what that meant.

Andy rolled over toward his wife. He liked thinking that he had a wife. A woman whom he loved, who loved him back, who would be there for him, who would take care of him and for whom he could provide. And he didn't have to worry if he was every going to get laid again.

Andy was up and raring to go. It was just after eight on his watch, but then, he hadn't changed it to Pacific Time. Dana rolled over and glanced at the clock on the night table, and squinting, was barely able to make out ten minutes after five. She had either adjusted to California time, or she was hungover, or both.

"What are you doing up so early?" She knew, so she didn't wait for an answer. "Nobody this side of the Rockies is up yet. You probably can't even get a cup of coffee in the lobby yet." She put a pillow over her head and rolled over to try to go back to sleep.

Andy was sitting at the desk with maps and brochures spread out. "I can't sleep, so I'm going to try to map out our day." He picked up the biggest of the maps, rustled it to flatten it out, and then pressed it out on top of the pile on the desk.

Dana cringed at the noise. At least he wasn't bothering her, she thought. At least he was letting her sleep in a little. She curled up around one of the plush pillows and closed her eyes, trying desperately to return to slumber, her head pounding.

Andy opened the desk drawers, one after the other, looking for something on which to write, and a pen. He jumped up from the chair and went over to the suitcase, which was now sitting precariously on the edge of the dresser. He unzipped it quickly, but caught his finger. "Ouch." He tried to be quiet, but he had drawn blood. He put his finger in his mouth and with the other hand, rifled through the suitcase. He knew there was a notepad in there, because Dana said she was going to journal about the trip. He pulled out a pile of clothes, and with it came a flurry of confetti. "What the hell?" This time, he forgot to be quiet.

"Geez, Andy." Dana half woke up. "What are you doing over there?" She was up on her elbows. "What is all that?"

"I have no idea. It's all over your suitcase."

Dana squinted again. Andy was trying to do all of this by the dim light coming from the bathroom, and the door was only open a few inches. "Oh man, my mother." By now, she was sitting upright in the bed. "My mother did that. She told me her sister did it to her when she went away for her honeymoon. I forgot all about it." Dana dropped back into the pillows. "I'll clean it up later."

Andy found what he was looking for, and began work on the itinerary for the day. Within minutes, Dana was breathing evenly, having fallen back into a deep sleep.

"Okay, it's time to get up!" Andy announced while kicking the door of the Honeymoon Suite closed behind him, carrying two cups of coffee. He had put the finishing touches on the itinerary, showered, gotten dressed, and then explored the hotel lobby. It was already almost seven, this time, California time, and he was anxious to get the day moving.

Dana wasn't any more looking forward to getting out of bed than she was two hours prior. Her head was pounding. Her taste for champagne was definitely diminishing. She rolled over to find Andy standing over her with a cup of coffee, steaming, and a single yellow rose.

"Good morning honey."

Dana smiled. "Good morning." She squirmed up to a sitting position, reached for the coffee and leaned up for a kiss. "Love you."

Andy turned on his heels, walked into the bathroom, and came out with a glass, half full, in which he had deposited the rose. "Don't get too excited. I lifted it from an arrangement in the lobby when nobody was around."

"It's the thought that counts!" Dana took a sip of the coffee and inhaled the steam. "Mmmmm. Nothing nicer than a sip of that first morning coffee."

"Well, hurry up. Breakfast starts at seven, and I've booked us for a bus tour of the Muir Woods." Andy took his cup and the newspaper, and deposited himself on the armchair by the window. Normally, he would watch Dana get up and get undressed for the shower, but he didn't feel a sense of urgency anymore. After all, she was his wife. He felt great comfort in that.

Dana dragged herself out of bed and carried her coffee and her clean underwear into the bathroom. Her intention was not to give Andy the opportunity to engage himself in her naked body. After all, there was an agenda to keep. That was the reason. Yep, that's it. She closed the bathroom door behind her.

Dana reached in and turned on the shower. While she waited for the hot water, she glanced at herself in the mirror. What have I gotten myself into, she thought. My first day of a honeymoon vacation and this man had me up at four in the morning. Her eyes were puffy ... too puffy for someone her age. She took a sip of her coffee, slipped out of her nightgown, and stepped into the shower.

"Want the window seat?" Andy could hardly contain himself. He was like a little boy when it came to things like this.

Dana, on the other hand, was not enthralled with the idea of a bus ride through the hills of northern California, and had no desire to look out the window down a mountainside, especially if she couldn't see the road. "You take the window." It didn't help her state of mind any that the tour guide mentioned the tour bus that had missed a turn and went careening over the side. She spent more time with her eyes closed than open, until they reached their destination. The weather was beautiful, if not a little chilly. The trees were magnificent, and as the tour guide had told them, they were the most 'valubullist' wood in the world. Dana wondered how to spell that word. She was glad she hadn't tried to talk Andy out of this tour. He was so happy to be there. Her sights were set on the second half of the day, when they were supposed to stop at a vineyard and winery. "I need the inside seat." Dana forced her way in front of Andy, and led him down the aisle to their seats on the bus. She made a grandiose gesture, beckoning him to slide across to the window, and promptly plopped herself down into the aisle seat.

"Did I marry a control freak?" Andy asked with a smile.

"I'm not a control freak." Dana was mildly offended. "There are just a few things that bother me a little. You know I don't like to fly. I don't like heights. And I certainly don't like looking out the window of this bus over the hillside, especially when it's so close to the edge that I can't even see the road."

Dana wanted to continue. *I'm afraid of snakes, closed in places, escalators and elevators, bridges, crowds, and most men.* She thought better of it, particularly the last one. Her father was a very tough man, insensitive to her very emotional being. Her two brothers had never given her real reason to trust men. She hadn't ever really dated a guy like Andy before. All the others ever wanted was to get into her pants. Andy did too, but at least was willing to get to know and love her first.

"No problem. Just give me the camera." Andy situated himself and got ready to do his impression of Ansel Adams, although there was color film in the camera. He wasn't very good at framing the pictures, so Dana knew she would have to probably have enlargements printed and then crop them if there were any of them worth framing.

Dana closed her eyes as the bus driver swerved out of the parking lot and onto the highway. "Next stop is Snyder's Winery. This is a family owned vineyard, and has been for over eighty years. The Snyders were one of the first to settle up in this area, and have consistently refused to sell their small acreage to the larger companies." The bus driver continued, but all Dana heard was the word wine. It would help her get over the jitters she felt from riding the damn bus.

"That wasn't too bad, was it?" Andy squeezed Dana's hand to wake her. The ride had only taken forty-five minutes, yet she had been able to fall off to sleep. "The bus driver said there's a little luncheonette there so we can grab a bite before we take the tour."

They got off the bus and headed for the main building, along with all of the other tourists. Andy went straight to the desk to get the maps. This was his usual M.O. and had Dana affectionately referred to him as the camp counselor every time they went anywhere. He did, in fact, earn his Eagle Scout. That was the one thing he had in common with her father, and her grandfather for that matter. He asked at the desk about the tour schedules and the wine tasting times.

"Okay, here's the agenda."

"Really, Andy? Agenda?"

"Sorry. Just my nature." Andy continued. "We have time for lunch now, because the next tour is at two. The tour only takes about 50 minutes, and they have the wine tasting every half hour over there in that room." Andy pointed over Dana's shoulder to a room that looked very much like a wine cellar. She could only see the one wall, but it was floor to ceiling, wine racks.

"Sounds like a good *agenda.*" Dana smirked. She was only teasing Andy. She did that a lot. She walked away from him toward the cafeteria. "You coming?"

"Everything on here has cucumber or pickles in it." Dana made a face. The last thing she wanted was to have an allergic reaction on her honeymoon. She slapped the menu closed. "I'll just have some toast."

"You know, you can ask them to make it without the cucumbers.

Have a salad or a sandwich." Andy wished Dana would, for once, stand up for herself. He never understood how she can be a tiger in business, but she would eat a steak that was undercooked rather than sending it back to the kitchen to have it prepared the way she ordered it.

"I guess." She scanned the menu one more time just as the waitress arrived at the tableside.

"Where are you folks from?" Ava pulled a pen from behind her ear. Her nametag had food smeared on it, so Dana was already a little turned off.

"Atlanta," she said curtly. "May I have a chef's salad with no cucumbers and an iced tea, please?" Dana closed the menu and handed it to the waitress.

"I'll have a burger, rare, with fries and a coke, please." Andy looked at Dana. Her demeanor had changed and he didn't know why. "You okay?"

"Yeah, I'm fine. Just found it funny that there wasn't any wine on the menu."

Andy thought this was a joke. He laughed.

Though the tour was interesting enough, Andy and Dana both enjoyed the wine tasting. The sommelier was entertaining, and Dana loved the fact that there was a lot of audience participation. He blindfolded her and asked her to try to discern the difference between three kinds of wine, after she had had the opportunity to taste them with sight and explanation. All she knew is that was that she got six glasses, albeit small ones, of wine all to herself.

When the tasting was over, Andy and Dana agreed that there was one particular wine that they both really liked, and made arrangements to have a case shipped home. Dana picked up a small box of chocolates and a couple of ceramic wine stoppers to take back as gifts and to keep as mementos.

They boarded the bus once again, but this time, Dana offered to take the camera and the window seat. She was much more relaxed and didn't really care what the bus driver was saying. She laid the souvenir bag across Andy's lap as the bus pulled out onto the highway. He rested his hands on the bag, put his head back and closed his eyes. They were seated near the rear of the bus, and when most of the other passengers had settled in and either closed their eyes or engaged in reading or conversation, Dana slipped her hand under the bag and started teasing Andy. She settled her hand squarely between his legs.

"Whoa." Andy jumped. "What are you doing?

"Don't you know?" A devious grin came over Dana's face. "Here?" Andy almost looked panicked. "Can't you wait until we get back to the hotel?"

"Can you?" Dana gently began rubbing in a circular motion, while Andy did everything he could not to react. "A suggestion of things to come, my dear …"

Andy could hardly wait to get up to the room. He was unbuttoning his shirt as he forced the key into the hotel room door. Dana snickered at his fumbling. Then, she yawned.

When they finally got into the room, Dana went into the bathroom. When she came out, Andy was already in bed, stark naked, beckoning her. *I guess this is part of the deal when you're on a honeymoon*, she thought to herself. The bus ride and the wine had taken its toll on her libido. She undressed. He watched. That always made her feel uncomfortable, but it gave him pleasure, so she yielded.

She slipped under the covers and he was immediately on top of her. Andy was one of those, lovers who went straight in for the kill. There was little foreplay, and there was very little romance. Dana was beginning to understand that sometimes there was passion, or just lovemaking, or just plain fucking. She was figuring out that sex had different roles in a relationship. She never knew which one she was going to get. Andy didn't really have a very clear delineation. She responded to him, this time, lustfully. That's the wine talking, she thought. Grinding her body against his always gave him the idea she was enjoying herself.

Andy rolled off of her, panting and sweating. "Whew." He let out a huge sigh. That was the signal. It was time for his nap. He rolled toward her and kissed her gently. "Love you honey." He fell back into the pillow and closed his eyes. Dana thought, they make a lot of jokes about this, but he really does just roll over and go to sleep.

Dana got up, went into the bathroom and took a shower. They were supposed to go to the Top of the Mark Hopkins Hotel for crab claws and champagne, but that wasn't for another two hours. After a long, relaxing shower, she curled up in the chair by the window with that journal she was supposed to be keeping, and began jotting down some notes. She hadn't written anything since they got on the plane in Atlanta. She was so hopeful then.

She still is.

Dana was much better at creeping around the room than Andy had been. It was either that, or Andy was a deeper sleeper. She quietly picked up the phone and called down to the front desk. "Do you happen to know the dress code for the Top of the Mark?" she asked. Dana had heard from a few friends who had told her about it, and that people still got pretty dressed up.

"The Top of the Mark requests tie and jacket for the gentlemen," came a voice from the other end of the line. "Definitely order the crab claws and champagne."

"That was what we planned on doing" Dana smiled. Everyone she told about her honeymoon had mentioned this. She was looking forward to the panoramic view of the city of San Francisco from the top of this famous hotel. Andy had put it in his agenda, begrudgingly, having had Dana force his hand. But when he looked at the other things that he wanted to accomplish, it turned out to be fine with him, because the timing worked perfectly and the location was right where they needed to be to board the bus for their "San Francisco by Night" tour. "Thanks very much."

Dana hung up the phone and quietly strolled over to the bedside. *He's so cute when he's sleeping,* she thought. She leaned over and, brushing aside a few wisps of hair, gently kissed him on the forehead. "Time to get up," she whispered. "We have about forty-five minutes to get ready and grab a cab. I spoke to the desk. You have to wear a tie."

"Ugh." Andy ground his palms over his eyes and reached for his glasses. "We could save time and shower together."

"I've already showered. You've been out for over an hour."

"Okay, then, do we have time for anything else?"

"We have a lifetime ahead of us for that. Get up and get moving." Is that all he ever thinks about? Dana walked over to the suitcase. "We should really hang some of this stuff up." She pulled out some more of the clothes and another flurry of confetti flew out, gently drifting to the floor. Dana threw her head back and looked up at the ceiling. "Marge, I'm gonna kill you."

Andy was already in the shower by the time Dana had cleaned up what was now the third mess from the confetti. She slipped into an A-line dress and sandals, and sat on the edge of the armchair, waiting for her husband. She giggled to herself. Husband. What a strange word.

The San Francisco air was brisk. It wasn't winter, but there was a definite chill in the air. She was thinking maybe she should run back upstairs and get a jacket. Andy had already hailed the cab and was motioning her to climb in.

"Mark Hopkins Hotel, please." Andy said confidently. He sat back and looked out the window. He lifted his arm up around Dana's shoulder and pulled her close. "I just love this. I love you."

No man she had ever known had made her feel so comfortable, so safe. Andy had a lot of big dreams and aspirations, but the one thing Dana loved about him the most was that he made her feel safe, happy and loved. Sometimes, Andy was a little too stoic, conservative and stubborn in his thinking. The other side of Andy, though, was that he made her laugh: not just at jokes, but at him, at herself and at life itself. It was a very freeing feeling to be able to do that ... to not take everything so seriously. Dana thought that might just be more important than anything. She wanted to get better at that.

Before she had even gotten the chance to panic at this cabbie's driving, they were there. They climbed out and at the exact same moment, looked up. It was an old hotel. Dana read somewhere that it had opened in 1926. When they walked in the lobby, they were overwhelmed by its lavish beauty. Andy went over to the desk to ask his usual twenty questions. Dana strolled around the lobby, taking in the art, accoutrements, rugs and furniture. During her investigation, she discovered the elevators, next to which there stood a sign that read "Top of the Mark Restaurant, 19th floor."

Andy was almost trotting over to Dana. "19th floor." Dana stepped to the side, and revealed the sign. "Oops," Andy said. "I guess I could lighten up a little." He reached over and pushed the up button for the elevator. "We didn't need a reservation just for the bar, and since we're kind of early, we probably will be able to get a window table. The guy at the desk told me I should tell them we're on our honeymoon … might get us a free glass of champagne."

There it was again. Andy was too into bargains. He was almost blatant about looking for free things and discounts. It was sometimes a little embarrassing. There must be a reason for it, she thought.

"Look, even the elevator has a chandelier." Dana was trying hard to enjoy the experience but here they were, again, in an old building in an old elevator. The ride, though, was seamless, and the doors opened on the 19th floor to reveal a magnificent view. They only had to walk a few steps from the elevator bay to be able to see the San Francisco skyline. They were seated right by the window and could see the Transamerica pyramid building among a few other landmarks.

"Is that the Golden Gate Bridge?" Dana strained to see through the fog in the distance.

"It could be. Or it could be the bridge that goes to Oakland." Andy always had an answer. Even if he didn't know the answer, he always offered one. Dana was trying to figure out if this was a man thing or an Andy thing.

Before Dana even got her purse situated, the server was at their table, placing an open, chilled mini-bottle of champagne down, along with two glasses. "Compliments of the house. Congrats on the marriage." Can I get you two lovebirds anything else?"

Dana knew that Andy had called ahead. Or maybe had asked the front desk do it. She blushed, a little, but not much. After all, this is why she came to the Top of the Mark. "Do you have a menu? Everyone told us we should have the crab claws. Is it an appetizer kind of thing?"

"Yep. Everyone does that. It's what we're famous for, I guess." "Is that the Golden Gate Bridge?" Andy asked.

"I have no idea. I've only been here two weeks. I'm from Manhattan." The waitress turned on her heels and headed back toward the kitchen.

"Oh well," Andy recoiled. "And look at some of those guys… wearing jeans and polo shirts. I thought you said I had to wear a tie and jacket."

"Hey. I only told you what I was told."

"So again, my favorite quote from Alfred E. Neuman comes into play."

"Who the hell is that? " Dana interrupted.

"Oh my, you mean I married an infidel? Don't you know who Alfred E. Neuman is?" Andy had a pained expression on his face and Dana really thought she had missed something important in her education. "And you're supposed to be well educated?"

"Alfred E. Neuman is the mascot of Mad Magazine. And he said, and I quote, 'the more you cultivate mankind, the more clods you turn up.'"

Dana relaxed her shoulders. She really should have known better. Andy's choice of literature was definitely not the same as hers. She picked up her glass to toast, "Here's to Alfred E. Neuman, in all his wisdom." They touched their glasses just as the waitress placed a large platter of crab claws, complete with dipping cups full of mustard, butter and something Dana didn't recognize in front of them. "Here's to Alfred, and here's to San Francisco, and here's to us!"

Andy tapped his glass against hers and took a sip. Dana sipped hers as well. She was taking it slow with the champagne today.

The sunset was magnificent. Dana took several pictures. Some were of Andy, but most were of the sunset on the bay. This was one of her favorite things to do. Photography. In fact, that's one of the reasons she got her first job out of college. "What time do we have to leave?"

"We have to pick up the bus at 7:00, but it's only a few blocks away. We can leave now and walk, or we can stay a little while and catch a cab. Up to you."

"Let's stay, and then take a cab. I think we're going to be doing enough walking later." Dana imagined herself trying to walk up and down those city blocks in her sandals. They were long blocks and likely hills. They were nowhere near Lombard Street, but still. She was looking forward to dinner in Chinatown, but wasn't too happy about boarding another bus for another tour. All she could think of was that in a few days, they were taking that Parlour Car Tour thing down the Pacific Coast Highway to Los Angeles. She was not looking forward to that at all, although she had been told she would have a blast with her camera.

"Great. Want another glass of champagne? There's a little left in the split."

"Let's do that. Split it."

"Wait for me. Let me use the ladies room before we go." She started toward the corner and turned. "You know what? Don't. Here, take the camera."

"Okay. I'll go down ahead and hail a cab." Andy stepped into the elevator and Dana went into the ladies room. Typical of him to go on ahead and not wait, she thought. He always goes on ahead.

As she turned the corner of the hallway entry into the stall area her jaw nearly dropped. This is exquisite, she thought. *A pleasant enough place to pee. That's what Andy would say.* She smiled as she rinsed her hands and reached for a towel. *Wow! Linen towels.* She wasn't sure if she was supposed to tip the lady who handed one to her. Dana reached into her purse, opened her wallet and slipped out a single dollar bill. She handed it to the lady in the French maid's uniform, and the lady nodded.

Dana pushed the button for the elevator and waited. The restaurant was very crowded and noisy. She was ready to leave. The doors opened, and yet another young newlywed couple walked out. She was only guessing this because the girl was wearing a slightly wilted corsage, like the one she had worn on the flight yesterday, but had left back in the hotel room.

Dana stepped into the elevator alone.

Andy stepped out of the elevator and stopped at the desk. "Do I need to call a cab?"

"No sir," replied the reception clerk. "Our doorman will hail one for you. It shouldn't take but a minute or two."

"Thanks." Andy was almost skipping toward the door of the hotel. He loved the revolving door at "The Mark" because it was so high. He would have gone around and around in it a few times if he had been about twenty years younger.

He tipped the doorman and then stood next to the door to watch for Dana. He slightly lost his balance and fell back against the wall. *I didn't have that much to drink,* he thought.

"Sir, please move away from the building and come down by the street."

"Got the cab?" Andy asked.

"Not yet sir. I believe we just had a mild tremor." The doorman was asking everyone to move away from the side of the building.

"I have to go get my wife." Andy was panicked.

"I'm sorry sir. You can't reenter the building." The doorman extended his arm across Andy's chest. "It's probably nothing. Just wait here. I'm sure she'll be down soon."

The elevator doors were closed. Dana had lost her balance at the same moment, and had thought the same thing. "I made sure not to have too much champagne," she said out loud to nobody. She peeled herself away from the elevator wall, and pushed the button marked "L" again, as if that would make the elevator move faster.

There was a sudden jolt, followed by sudden darkness. Dana dropped her purse and plastered her hands against the wall. She opened her mouth to scream, but nothing came out, as if she were yawning. She could feel her heart pounding in her throat but she suddenly couldn't remember how to take in a breath.

Unexpectedly, the elevator car jerked and plunged, stealing Dana from the floor. What seemed like forever was a split second. She thought to herself, *is this what they mean when they say you see your whole life before your eyes just before you die?* She kept her hands plastered to the wall, although her feet weren't on the floor. The car suddenly stopped its free fall. Dana crumpled down and smacked her head on the arm rail, slithering down into a heap on the floor of the now steady and silent elevator car. She lay motionless.

All around her, the building shook. People were screaming and trampling each other as they scrambled for the stairs. The restaurant was empty within thirty seconds. The young lady with the wilted corsage led the way holding onto a lighter, while others gathered candles from the tables as they tripped down the stairs. The crowd grew with each level of the floor.

Andy watched frantically from the sidewalk as crowds of people burst through the two side doors of the front of the hotel and out onto the street. Too many people had tried to use the revolving door and they were stuck, so they had to back up and let some out back into the hotel lobby. No Dana.

Emergency sirens blared from all directions. Then there was another huge rumble, knocking people off their feet in the streets. Andy and Dana's waitress was holding onto a light pole when he heard her screaming. "For this I left New York." Just next to her, she noticed a small crack in the sidewalk. "Was that there? Was that there? Is that new? Is this going to open up and swallow us?"

A complete stranger went over to her and put his arm around her. "Hang in there, sister." We go through this a lot, although this one is a little bigger than most." He took a deep breath. "You'll be okay."

The numbers of people exiting the building was dwindling. Still no Dana. Andy went back up to the doorman. "My wife is still in there. I have to go in and find her."

"Sorry sir." The doorman was adamant. "Nobody goes in there now until the police and fire check the building and we get an all clear. If she's still in there, they'll find her."

Andy stepped back for a second and then changed his mind. "Is there another exit where they might be evacuating?"

Starting to be a little unnerved by the whole situation, the doorman was also beginning to get frustrated with all of Andy's questions. He knew the guy was worried, but there were hundreds of people with whom he had to concern himself. "Look, fella. You could walk around the back to the service entrance if you want, but I doubt she came out there."

Andy had no idea what to do. So, like everyone else, he waited. Inside the hotel, inside the elevator, Dana was out cold. From all appearances, she could have been dead. There was a tiny trickle of blood coming from her right ear, and she was breathing slow, shallow breaths, but she was breathing. Her purse had spilled out all over the floor of the elevator, which was now suspended between the third and fourth floors of the Mark Hopkins Hotel in San Francisco.

As she lay there, her mind took her to a different dimension. *Thiswas how it was going to end. After all they had been through; this washow it was going to end.*

PART 2

CHAPTER 6

Dana tried as hard as she could to rouse herself. She felt as though she had melted into the couch, or the bed, or wherever it was that she was in such a deep sleep. She felt as though she had been hit by a bus. She's done this before. When she was younger, it happened all the time after a particularly intense sports practice or game. Now though, it happened more often than not when she had been drinking. *"I didn't think I had that much to drink tonight,"* she thought to herself. *"Andy is waiting for me, but I can't seem to shake out of this."* "Wake up! Dana? Wake up!" Andy tried to rouse his wife of 23 years. "If we're going to go, we need to leave now." Andy was short of patience. This was not a new circumstance, and he was getting a little tired of it.

Dana was in a fog, again. She had gotten dinner on the table, rushed through the dishes, and took the opportunity to close her eyes for a few minutes. She really wasn't looking forward to this, probably a result of having had too much to drink, again. She just wanted to sleep. Andy had convinced her that they should work on their marriage. He has been unhappy and didn't really understand what was wrong, so he had arranged an appointment with a marriage counselor. Dana was skeptical, but if it would keep him off her case, she would go.

"If I don't like this woman, I'm not going back," she said as they got into the car. "Where did you find this person, anyway?" "I found her in our Provider List. I spoke to her when I made the appointment. She has twenty years experience." Andy stared straight ahead as he drove. "Look, if you don't like her we can find someone else. Don't you think it's worth trying? I mean are you happy with the way things are?"

Dana didn't answer. *How much had he told her? What did he know? Did this lady already have an opinion about her?* Dana wished she had taken a quick hit from her bottle before they left.

There was silence in the elevator. They didn't even make eye contact. Dana knew their marriage was in trouble. She knew Andy was right. She did not, however, have any idea of what was going on in his head. She never did. Andy had proven to be, over the years, a very stoic and unemotional man. The only time he was reactive was with the kids. She found herself getting so frustrated with him because it seemed as though he didn't hear her. He might have seemed to be listening, but as soon as whatever it was that was said blew over, he would revert back to the way things were, as if nothing had ever happened.

Dana was, at the very least, curious to see what Andy would say to this lady.

"I feel like nothing but a paycheck." Andy sat stoically in the armchair, directly facing the therapist. He didn't want to make eye contact with Dana, because he thought that the things he was saying would make her angry. Actually, he wanted to make her angry so she would finally at least talk to him.

Dana was listening, but under her breath, she was laughing. *A paycheck? Really? If that's what you feel like, you must have really low self-esteem, because you're not a very good paycheck, at least not lately.* Dana was exhausted from trying to hold together

her job, her home and her family, while Andy went about his business going to work from 9-5 and coming home, waiting for his dinner, and then watching television all night. She had been the bread-winner for the last few years because he was struggling so much professionally. What made Dana so angry was that he seemed to be okay with that. He wouldn't admit to being in a depression himself, so he wouldn't seek help. *Isn't that just like a man?* It always amazed Dana how she could have this long involved conversations in her head in a split second.

The therapist urged him to continue. "I would say 'how does that make you feel' but I assume you would laugh at me, expecting that from a therapist." She smiled. "That has to take a blow at your feelings."

"She doesn't talk to me. I don't really know how she feels. She pulls away when I try to touch her."

"Dana, is that true?" Carmen was trying everything she could to engage Dana in the conversation, but she had the suspicion that Dana was somehow not on the same spiritual plane. Dana was bobbing her head. It wasn't in agreement. Carmen wondered if she was taking some kind of medication or had been drinking. At this point, she wasn't going to be of much help in the session. There was something missing from this woman, but she couldn't quite put her finger on it.

"I guess so."

"Any idea why?"

"No." Dana squirmed in her seat. "Are we done yet?" She wanted to get out of there and get home before him so she could get another drink.

"Dana, we haven't even started. If you really want to work on your relationship with Andy, you have to participate a little." Carmen didn't know these two very well yet. This was only the first time they worked together. There were a lot of basic questions and answers that followed, and Carmen watched each one of them like a hawk, looking for nuances and reactions, trying to read these two very unique individuals.

"Okay, so here's what I'd like to do. I'd like to see each one of you separately a few times before the three of us meet again. It seems as though you both have things you want to say, but don't know how to do so in front of the other." She slid her chair closer to her desk and reached for her calendar.

Appointments made, the two stood up in unison. "Thank you," Dana said half-heartedly. This was Andy's idea. She wasn't too sure of this lady. She laughed at stupid things. Maybe she was just as nervous as they were. They had been through this before when Dana was having problems with anxiety and panic, but that was fifteen years ago.

"See you both next week. Wait, Dana you on Tuesday and Andy, you on Wednesday." They walked out silently. He waited for the elevator, she took to the stairs. Dana almost tripped trying to get down and out of the building and to the car. She knew he would methodically walk to the car, get in, adjust his mirrors, start the car, and set the radio to some kind of sports or news and then slowly pull out. She would have been halfway home by then.

When they pulled up to the house, she jumped out of the car. All three of the kids were in the den watching a movie, so she was able to sneak back into the bedroom unnoticed. She ripped open her closet door and fumbled around the shelf underneath the sweaters until she found the unopened pint bottle of whiskey she had hidden there earlier. She opened it and quickly downed half of it. Screwing the lid back on, she threw her head back and closed her eyes, as if to savor the taste. She didn't give a shit about the taste. She needed the action, the relaxing feeling. She needed to be able to drop her shoulders from the tension. She needed to feel the warmth of the alcohol as it traveled down her insides. Most importantly, she needed to steel herself for the inevitable fight that would occur when Andy came in.

"Yoo hoo … where did you go?" Andy acted as if there was nothing wrong. "How did you get back there so fast?" He came directly back to the bedroom, too, tossing his jacket on the bed and loosening his tie. "Are you okay?"

Dana had barricaded herself in the bathroom. "I'm in the bathroom, do you mind?" She had taken the bottle with her, and as she sat bare-bottomed on the toilet, she poured the rest of it down her throat, trying to force herself to urinate, so it would at least sound like she belonged in there.

"Geez." Andy said under his breath. "I was just asking." Unfortunately for Andy, he talked to himself under his breath a lot, but didn't know how to do it quietly. There were many times we he said things out loud that he didn't mean for anyone to hear, but some people did. Especially his wife.

Dana came out of the bathroom and passed right by Andy without acknowledging him. She had already put on her pajamas, and was headed down the hall to go see the kids.

"Is that it?" Andy called after her. "Aren't we even going to talk about what happened tonight?" His frustration with her was mounting. He had no clue why she was ignoring him. What did he do that was wrong? Or what hadn't he done? He was lost.

That session was good for one thing, Dana thought. She had now figured out the best way to keep Andy oblivious to her drinking. He was, after all, a man. Getting sex was his main goal in life. This would solve the problem. Dana, based on her previous experiences with men, believed that. Even most of the gay guys she knew were enamored with their penises. Dana would now somehow seduce Andy whenever the kids weren't around, if she was sober enough. She'll probably even do it when they were home if she was drunk enough. When they were in the car, she would reach over and tease him.

He would half-heartedly tell her to stop. When they were at the table, she would stretch her leg out and wiggle her foot up between his legs. Her favorite thing to do was to catch him off guard in public, and watch him try to control himself until they got home.

After a while, Dana would be waking up naked in bed, with her clothes all over the floor, every other night. She would pounce on him anytime, anywhere, as long as she could keep him away from her bottles.

She was sure this would work.

Dana couldn't believe a week had passed so quickly. She couldn't remember much of what went on, but yet she found herself in the therapist's tiny little office again. It was her turn. Andy had been there last night. He was extremely closed mouth when he got home, in fact even a little aggressive, Dana thought. "Don't ask me what we talked about. It's none of your business," he said.

"I think my husband thinks that everything I do and say is about him. He never, for a second, lets in that maybe I feel the way I do for other reasons ... not because he said or did something wrong." Dana started out the session with an explosive revelation. "I hate him." She paused for a few uncomfortable seconds. "I didn't mean that. I'm in hate with him, how's that?"

"Pretty strong language," Carmen replied. "Any idea where this comes from?"

"I'm not too pleased with men in general." Dana was on a tear. "Andy thinks the only way I show him affection is in the bedroom. Doesn't see the thousand other things I do and say to show him I love him and care for him." Dana started thinking back. "It's all about sex. Always has been." For every guy she's ever known.

Dana was frozen in thought...

"Get off of me!" Dana screamed. "Get off!" Dana tried to wriggle out from underneath Kenny. He had her pinned down on his bed and his dorm room was locked. He was pulling at her collar, trying to get it below her bra. He was in a drunken stupor; she didn't even think he knew her name. She was drunk too, and the room was spinning.

Dana's badge of honor, being able to drink most of those guys under the table, might just have to be relinquished. She knew she was still on the third floor of her dorm, and she was pretty sure she could make her way back to her room. She was doing her best to fend him off, pulling at his arm with both of her hands. She finally was able to lift her right leg from under the weight of his torso and knee him in the thigh. "Whassa madder?" Kenny rolled over and finally let her up. "I was just having a lill fun. We can fool arown. Nobodyull know." Dana originally thought Kenny was a nice guy ... and kind of cute. She wondered if he would still look cute to him in the morning if she gave it up to him. She was still a virgin. Maybe he didn't know that. Maybe he didn't care. Just another horn toad, she thought.

"I need to go. I'm gonna be sick." She tumbled off of the bed and onto the floor. Getting up as quickly as she could, she stumbled toward the door. Dana lost her balance and fell into the closet. She could barely see, but the smell of the shoes and dirty clothes was sobering enough to motivate her to get up. Guys are disgusting, she thought. She found the door, fumbled with the lock, and she was free, slamming the door behind her. She heard him calling.

"Wait. Wait." She paused. Then there was silence. She opened the door ever so slightly and peeked back in. Kenny was out cold, his pants around his knees and he was sprawled halfway on the bed and halfway on the floor. Dana quietly reclosed the door, straightened her blouse, and instead of going back to the party, headed the other direction down the hallway to the stairwell exit.

Once through the doors, she collapsed against the wall, in tears. Rape, she thought to herself. That would have been rape. I don't even know the guys last name. Why did he think just because I had a little beer I would want to have sex with him? Her heart was pounding. I hate guys, she thought to herself. All they want is sex. It's all about sex. Nothing else. Next time, I might not be so lucky. Tears barely trickled down her face. But they were there. She recognized the feeling of fear, but she also felt anger, both at Kenny and at herself. Alcohol may just have done her in. What if she had taken one more beer and couldn't defend herself? What if she let him have his way and she didn't remember? What if she got pregnant?

A familiar feeling came over her, one that she, knew too well, unfortunately. She began to salivate, and she knew she had to move quickly, but had made a bad decision leaving the building on the men's side. Dana stumbled down the stairs. Three flights never seemed that long before. She tripped down the last few steps and dove for the door, slamming against it. She landed halfway in the building, but her upper body was laying halfway outside. Her cheek was lying on the sidewalk and she could feel gravel next to her eye. All of a sudden, it seemed like everything she had eaten or had to drink came roaring up from below and flying out of her mouth with such force, like a missile, that it landed several yards in front her. And it kept coming. Dana managed to pull herself to her knees and crawled over to the side of the doorway, making every attempt to aim toward the bushes.

She hated guys. Isn't there anything more to having a boyfriend than having sex?

She was back in the room with Carmen. Shaking.

"That's not the first time something like that happened ..."

Dana was starting to open up a little more with Carmen. She had battled with the committee in her head her whole life. She had finally become weary of the anxiety, the depression, the mood swings. She was really ready to get to the bottom of things, fix them and move on. She had sought professional help long before she ever met Andy, but she wasn't willing to be honest, didn't like the labels given to her, and really wasn't ready to heal … from anything. She recalled the Dr. in college, and some lady she saw for a little while before she really started dating Andy.

Carmen was different. She didn't take any shit from Dana. She had patience, but didn't allow herself to be manipulated. Dana had become very good at doing and saying things just for reactions.

In fact, Dana really didn't know how she felt about anything anymore. She had no opinions, no particular feelings one way or the other; she was numb. When things got uncomfortable, she took whatever action she had to, to make herself more emotionless, and when she got too numb, she made herself feel. Pain: A burn, a cut; anything to snap her out of it. Or, she would pick fights with Andy to have a reason to slam out of the house and go get more liquor.

"So, there was this one time I … um," she started. "Never mind, it's not important." Dana had her arms crossed and was pinching the insides of her arms. She did that a lot, especially when she was talking about things that made her uncomfortable.

"Okay, whenever you're ready," Carmen reassured her. "And Dana, you don't have to tell me if you don't want to."

"It was a dream." She lied. It was actually a flashback to something that happened to her as a teenager. She tried to shake loose of the feeling, but every time she closed her eyes, she pictured herself standing in the souvenir shop, holding a snow globe of Stone Mountain. Out of nowhere, an older black man came up from behind her a cupped his hand on her crotch, rubbing back and forth. For a split second, she didn't know what to do, but as fast as he started, he was gone.

Dana was frozen. She stood there, turned and looked for him, but he was quickly out of sight. She noticed, though, a slight feeling of warmth between her legs. Was she normal? What was that? She was scared, but somehow, excited.

She had made the decision not to tell anyone. She should have done something right then and there, but as usual, Dana was too full of fear to stand up for herself. Once again, she let it happen to her. At fourteen, she couldn't stand up for herself and she still can't at forty four.

Dana gathered herself together and tried to begin again. Nobody ever took her seriously anyway. Every time she wanted to talk to her father, Ben was so busy thinking about what he was going to say next, he never listened to her words. He always made her feel like she had no voice.

Dana unfolded the story to Carmen, including the part about being excited by it. "It has been thirty years since this happened. So why am I still dreaming about it? Why do men do that? Can't they just leave girls alone and find a grown woman? Can't they just take care of themselves? I thought guys jerked off in the shower all the time anyway. What goes on in their heads that they have to do that to me?" This wasn't just a dream. She thought about it all the time.

"Let's explore this a little more next week." Carmen chose her words carefully. She really hated leaving Dana up in the air with issues as touchy as this but they had already gone for well over an hour. Dana slumped back into the couch. I can't go home to him, she thought. I don't want to go back to my real life. She had a pint bottle under the seat of the car. That would make it at least tolerable.

CHAPTER 7

Dana loved it when the company put on their holiday parties. She had an "in" with the planning committee. All she had to do was hitch a ride into work in the morning, and then volunteer to go over to the hotel early with them to help set up. She was always rewarded with a string of extra 'free drink' tickets, and she didn't have to worry about driving home, because Andy was meeting her there.

She got four from Lucy and four from Suzanne, plus the one she got as an employee. She knew at least two people who wouldn't be using theirs, and by the time employees and guests had started to arrive, she had already downed four whiskeys. Dana was glad that there were four different bars set up. The bartenders get a little suspicious if she shows up too often. They just never pour very much liquor in those tiny glasses. And they add so much damn ice.

Dana picked up her fifth drink on the way out to the lobby to look for Andy. He had called to say that traffic was bad and that he would be late. Not a problem for her. He was only coming to make it look good. After scanning the crowd with no success, Dana returned to the ballroom and began looking for someone else. She had, in her recent state of discord, with Andy, with work, with herself and with her life in general, started to seek out answers to questions that had been swimming around in her head. She put her glass down on the first table she came upon and walked out onto the dance floor.

There she was. Dana didn't know if this was a really dumb thing to do or not. She just knew that in her current state, she was overwhelmingly attracted to this girl. Or maybe it was just the idea of being attracted to a woman. Or maybe it was that she was just angry at Andy. Or maybe she really was gay. She hadn't thought about it in years, since her thing in college. It was possible that her marriage wasn't going to make it through all of this. Was it her fault? Was it because of her anger? Was it because of his deceit? Maybe this is something she really needed to talk to her therapist about.

Barbara was sitting at a table in the corner with three other women. Dana didn't know if she was even interested in women. She just knew that she was single. She paused before going any further into the room and thought to herself. 'Am I unconsciously trying to find the tenderness I had with Michelle? Am I really going to make a move here?' Her mind kept throwing out questions as she slowly made her way across the room. She could feel the flutters in her stomach and her heart racing. "Am I really doing this?" she actually said out loud.

"Doing what?" Andy came up behind her.

"Uh … Um," Dana was so startled she couldn't think of anything to say. She was glad she had put her glass down. "Did you get a drink ticket?" She asked the question innocently, while reaching in her dress pocket. "Here's mine. Can you go over to the bar and get us some drinks while I look for a table?"

Dana put her purse down a table in the back of the room on the far corner, away from where Barbara was sitting. She didn't want to be tempted to stare. The last thing she needed was for Andy to notice. Oh, who am I kidding, she thought to herself. He doesn't notice anything, for God's sake. He wouldn't notice if I dyed my hair purple. The event droned on. Dana stole away from the table using the ladies' room or having a cigarette as an excuse until she methodically downed the rest of her free drinks. "Mind buying me another drink?" She asked Andy. Andy got up from the table and sought out the bar with the shortest line. This irritated Dana, because by the time he decided which line to get in, he could have waited at the nearest one, purchased the drink and had been back at the table. He's such a pain in the ass sometimes, she thought. It never dawned on her to be thankful that he was the one getting up to get her the drink. Being grateful was not in her repertoire these days.

They were silent in the car on the way home. Dana was extremely far gone, but she knew that she had to stay in the moment or there would be questions. When she reached over and put her hand on Andy's thigh, he winced.

"Not while I'm driving."

"What's wrong?"

"Let's just get home."

Dana sat back in her seat. Her heart was now thumping in her chest. There's nothing like panic to sober her up. *What does he have on his mind? Did someone tell him about the drink tickets? Was there something wrong at home? With the kids? His job?* Her mind was swirling, and now her stomach began to do the same.

"Uuuuuuhhhhhh." Dana sat up in her seat. "We may need to stop. I think I ate something that's not agreeing with me."

"Want me to pull off here?" They weren't in the best part of town, but Andy did not want her getting sick in his car. "What did you have?

"I ate some of that seafood. I know how long it had been sitting out. I was there when they set it up."

"Yeah, but it was on ice the whole time. Did it taste funny?"

"I don't know." She had to come up with something else. "Or maybe, something with some bad mayonnaise?" Dana belched, and that seemed to ward off the onslaught. "I'll be okay. Let's just go home."

Andy pulled into the driveway and roughly shifted the car into park, jolting Dana from her state of euphoric sleep. "We're here."

Dana rolled her head around to the front and shook it gently, reached over for the door handle and pushed open the door. Then she swung her legs over, rocked three times to get up the momentum to stand. Andy was already at the front door with the key in the lock.

"Come on." He was impatient. He was always impatient when someone was holding him up, Dana thought. He never noticed how many times we all had to wait at the front door for him. Just another example, she thought, of how he never looks beyond how things affect him directly. That's why he has that acid tongue. That's why he can go about his business as if nothing's wrong, even if his wife and children are a mess.

"I'm coming." Dana wasn't stumbling. She was careful not to let on how much she had to drink. She was doing a remarkable job of disguising her drinking. It was always, "I'm tired," or "I don't feel well." But she knew she was on a tightrope. This was her life every night. And tomorrow, she feared, she would have to somehow recover from tonight's festivities quickly, because she had an early production meeting.

The house was quiet. Not even the dog woke up. All three of the kids were in bed, asleep. Dana took pride in the fact that her kids were generally good kids. They all did well in school, were active in clubs and teams, had nice friends, and could be trusted to make good decisions, most of the time. Tonight was testament to the fact that despite her spiral downward, she wasn't hurting them or anyone else. Just herself.

Andy went straight to the den, opened up a cabinet in the bar and pulled out two of the big liquor bottles: his scotch and Dana's Jack Daniels. "You've been doing a lot more drinking these days."

Dana went over and looked at the two bottles. "Mine isn't much lower than yours." She backed away. "We both know I drink a little more than you." What Andy didn't know was that when she got too far ahead of him, she would take out his bottle and take a few gulps of the scotch to "help him catch up." She hated the taste of scotch. It's what her father used to drink. Just the smell of it made her think of him and how she hated the fact that he had created such a monster in her.

Andy took a deep breath. "I just want to be sure you aren't doing what you were doing a few years back when I found those empties under the sink."

Here came another flat out lie. "Of course not." Dana turned on her heels, but too fast, and lost her balance, falling into the wall. Trying to make light of it, she asked "Has that wall always been there?"

Andy didn't think it was funny. He went to sleep on the couch in the den.

"I believe in the sanctity of marriage, so I'm willing to work on it if you are. I'm not ready to throw away 23 years of marriage so easily." Dana was not pleased that she was the only one keeping her appointments with Carmen. "You have to put an effort into it too. I'm not the only one contributing troubling issues to this marriage."

Andy shrugged his shoulders. He wasn't the one who was always picking fights and leaving for hours at a time. Yeah, so what. So he watched a lot of television at night. That's how he relaxed. Andy had this argument with Dana in his head all of the time. Every now and then, she would catch him talking out loud to himself, and then he would have to dance around and make up something about practicing talking to a difficult client. He really was tired of the tension between them.

There's a long story that goes with a 23 year marriage. There had been a lot of ups and downs. There were medical issues and miscarriages; there were three amazing kids; there was a lot of financial insecurity; there was an awful lot of stereotypical role-playing. Dana was starting to squawk about how everything has always been the way Andy wanted it. There was some dishonesty and breakdown of trust; there was a lot of fighting and resentment building up and there was a lot of drinking. Dana had that addictive personality, and there were a lot of things she didn't want to think about. Alcohol had always helped her forget.

She grabbed her purse. "Aren't you going to say anything?"
"Nothing to say, just that you're not gonna blame your drinking on me, that's for sure."

"Fine." Dana slammed the door behind her. She stomped out to her car, trying to remember if there was any whiskey left in the pint bottle in her glove compartment. She had tried not to have anything to drink, but he had gotten her good and angry and she wanted to calm down before going in to see Carmen.

CHAPTER 8

"I wasn't very popular in high school. I mean, when my parents decided to move us all to Atlanta, it was a really inopportune time to do it," Dana told Carmen. She really believed that this move came at a time when girls were first starting to have a real reason to have a friend, other than to have someone with whom to play with dolls or ride bikes. "My mother used to ride me all the time ..."

Dana reflected ...

"Why don't you call somebody and go out somewhere?" Marge was starting to get a little concerned. Dana had been moping around the house the whole school break. She hadn't been given any homework of consequence, so all she had been doing is sleeping in, snacking, reading and napping for the whole Christmas break.

"Nobody's around." Dana went into her room and slammed the door. That always made her mother cringe and she knew it. That's why she did it. Isn't it expected of 13 year olds? It's not her fault that they made her move away this year. She's only been here four months and barely has had a chance to make friends.

"Ben!" Marge called outside. Ben James was only halfway through shoveling the snow from the sidewalk. He hated snow. He hated being cooped up in the house. It was so seldom it snowed in Atlanta,

and he was half sorry he moved his family there. He could have made the big move. He could have taken them all the way out to southern California. Either way, it was a burdensome process, but it was either move or start over, and he didn't think he had it in him to do that.

"Almost done." He lied. "Give me ten more minutes."

"Lunch is ready."

"I told you not to do that. I told you ... GEEZ." This always pisses him off. He knew exactly what he wanted for lunch and he didn't want her bothering him about what he was eating. He finished up the minimum amount of shoveling so that nobody would slip, and headed back toward the house. He silently went in, sat down and ate the damn sandwich.

"Where's Dana?"

"Having one of her things."

"What is it this time?"

"I have no idea. Just brooding." Marge cleared his plate. "The kids are all due in around five. I thought we could just have a big Italian dinner." She piled the lunch dishes in the sink and turned to him waiting for an answer.

"Fine." If Ben was speaking in one word sentences, Marge knew he was angry.

"What's the matter? Did I do something?"

"You know what you did." He got up from the table and walked toward the back of the house, stopping by Dana's bedroom, and knocked gently on the door. "You okay, pussycat?" He was hoping to visit and spend a few minutes with his only daughter. This wasn't *because he loved being with her, but because he didn't want to talk to Marge. He was, again, overcompensating, trying to be the good Daddy. What a load of shit, Dana thought.*

Dana jumped. She was, in fact, okay. She was pleasuring herself. She had just discovered this new phenomenon recently. She did it as often as she could steal away. She couldn't stop thinking about it. She quickly pulled the covers over herself, and wiped her hand on the side of the bed, grabbing her book.

"I'm fine, Dad." She had to catch her breath. "I just want to be alone."

Ben was so used to hearing those words that it didn't faze him, in the least. He headed down the hallway to his bedroom for his usual Saturday afternoon nap, disguised as 'watching sports' or 'enjoying an old movie.'

Dana never understood why he didn't just admit to the fact that he had fallen asleep. If she could successfully sleep through her weekends, she would. In fact, napping was her favorite way to pass the time. That is, until she discovered how to pleasure herself. She didn't even know what the word masturbation was. She only knew that it felt good. It reminded her of the days when she and her neighborhood pal, Laurie and she would spend hours on the back patio of her house. They would hang, suspended from the pole structure that, in the summertime, would hold the yellow and white striped awning used for shade from the Vermont sun. If she pulled herself up just so, exerting just the right amount of pressure, she would get this glorious tingly feeling down there. So did Laurie. Dana was only five or six at the time, and had no idea what it was, but it felt good. Some days, the two girls would hang for hours, giggling and squealing until it hurt.

"Dana, where exactly are you going with this? Carmen asked. "I know there's a point somewhere." Dana's mind wandered back to that afternoon, *when a clanking, sputtering,* beat up van pulled up in front of the house. Like clowns climbing out of a car in a circus, seven college-aged young men unloaded themselves onto the sidewalk, stretching, belching and doing other things teenage boys did that Dana hated. She peered through the curtain of the living room. Two of these guys were her brothers, one was a cousin, and the other four were friends. Cute ones.

Dana glanced at herself in the mirror to be sure her hair didn't look ridiculous. She was certainly not the vain type, but she didn't want to look bizarre, just in case she could somehow break through the 'little sister syndrome.' From the minute she had any interest at all in boys, she realized there was no shortage of guys around. She had two brothers and they, unlike her, were very popular. There was always any number of cute friends hanging around the house. That was the good part of having older brothers. The bad part of having older brothers was that you were ALWAYS going to be the little sister, and therefore, untouchable.

"Dana, I could use some help in the kitchen." Marge was attempting to feed what could be considered an army: Seven teenage boys, Dana and Ben. She had two large pans of lasagna in the oven, a huge bowl of salad and a large basket of garlic rolls from Antonio's. Her boys love Antonio's rolls and her lasagna. She was pretty sure dinner would go over well. Dana rolled her eyes: another one of her usual behaviors that Marge and Ben had gotten used to. She went into the kitchen, picked up the pile of paper goods and set the table.

After dinner, the boys went to get beer. Their explanation was that they wanted to drive all the way down to Florida the day after tomorrow, so tonight would have to be the partying night. Ben was looking forward to the evening. He had a taste for beer, himself. He had no problem with the kids drinking at the house. Since they made the legal drinking age 18, six out of the seven qualified, and the one that didn't was his kid.

When they got back from the beer run (two cases), Ben suggested playing a drinking game. Since they were a little too naïve, they allowed Ben to teach them his college drinking game. Everyone, including Dana, played. Marge wanted nothing to do with it, and went back to bed.

Dana, it turned out, liked beer. It was a little fuzzy tasting at first, but she got used to it quickly. She also got light headed quickly, and really liked that feeling. The only thing she was unhappy about is that the boys were paying little or no attention to her. And she wasn't very good at the game, so she had to drink a lot.

Ben thought it was cute. All his kids were drunk. Dana's one brother took the dog for a walk in his underwear. The other one was puking all over the front lawn. She lost track of her cousin and his friends. They had all gone out back earlier. She thought they might be ... Uh Oh. She was salivating. Shit, she thought. Someone's in the bathroom. She spun around and dove into her room, stretching to grab her trash can. And there it was ... heaving not only the beer, but all of the Italian food into her little pink waste can.

When the bathroom was free, she stumbled in there, and it started all over again. She flushed twice, but she couldn't get rid of the smell. She was too far gone to realize that she had vomit all over her nightgown. Back in bed, despite the spinning of her furniture all around her, she fell asleep.

Dana wasn't quite sure what time anyone else had gotten up. She only knew she felt like shit, and everyone was around the table eating breakfast except her. They wanted to get an early start doing a little sightseeing downtown. Dana didn't know if she was invited to join them so she sat silently fiddling with her spoon. There was no way she could eat.

The rumble of the train underneath her wreaked havoc on her head and made her stomach feel like it was climbing ever so slowly *upwards. When it lurched to a stop, everyone around her jumped up and started to leave. Dana couldn't understand how they had so much energy, but she found a way to pull herself up with the bar across the seat in front her, and make her way down the aisle behind the seven boys.*

When they stepped out of the train into the terminal, Dana nearly tripped over a spilled can of beer, and the vomiting commenced again. No more drinking for me, she thought. It isn't worth it.

"I guess I was preoccupied with the fight Andy and I had before I came over here." Dana started. "Think he's finally catching on to my drinking."

"It's about time," said Carmen, relieved. She had, in the short time they had been working together, already figured out that Andy was kind of an ostrich. He wasn't a deep thinker, and he didn't notice what Dana called 'nuances.' "Are you telling me you're ready to take a small step to try to fix this?"

"Please don't go there," Dana begged. Dana had learned to numb herself to anything unpleasant. Now she was hooked. She knew it, Carmen knew it, and she was pretty sure Matt knew it. Even her son was more perceptive than Andy. "I need to go."

Dana sat by the door, glancing around the room, trying to find someone that even remotely resembled her, her background, her upbringing. She had little success. These were all people in jeans and tee shirts, none of them seemed to have jobs. They weren't like her. She had no reason to sit there. Somehow, though, she didn't want to get up. Would it be rude? She thought maybe after the guy at the table in the front was finished talking, she'd quietly get up and slip out the door.

"It's simple," he said. "But it isn't easy. You have to work at it and you have to want it." What the fuck was she doing sitting in an AA meeting anyway. I don't have a problem, she thought. I just drink more that Andy sometimes. So I have a little fun. So what. It isn't getting in the way of anything. I'm not hurting anyone. I haven't gotten in an accident, haven't lost my job, or gotten a divorce like all these people. Yet.

"Just remember what it says in more about Alcoholism. It's a progressive disease. It gets worse, never better." It was at that point that Dana got up and headed for the door. She had heard enough. She opened the door next to her and quietly left, but the door squeaked as it slowly closed and everyone looked up at her. Oh well, she thought. *I'll never see these people again. The hell with them. This was a bad idea, anyway.*

She opened the door of her car and got behind the wheel. Under the seat, she had concealed a pint bottle of whiskey. She slid it out and put it up between her legs as she started the engine. As she pulled out onto the boulevard, she reached down and carefully unscrewed the cap, tilting the bottle upwards so she wouldn't spill any. Never mind that she didn't want to get the smell in her car; she just didn't want to waste any.

When she reached the on ramp to the highway, she could finally get a swig, as there was no oncoming traffic and no car on either side. She took a big gulp as she accelerated. That's fine for them, she thought. *I don't need that shit. I can stop if I want to. I just don't want to. If they had to contend with my issues, they'd drink too.* She took another hit from the bottle, and looking down at it, realized that she had almost finished the pint bottle. Oh well, she thought, there's more where that came from.

When Dana reached her exit, she took her foot off the gas pedal and coasted onto the exit ramp, all the while tilting her head back with the bottle at her lips, trying to get the last drop out. With her left elbow, she adeptly pushed the window button and the window went down. Glancing in her rear-view mirror, she saw no one behind her, and she gently tossed the empty onto the median. Rolling the window back up, Dana hit the gas just enough to roll up to the red light.

Andy was already home, and so were the kids. They're probably wondering where she was. She jumped out of the car, grabbed her purse and her briefcase, popping a piece of gum in her mouth and ran up the stairs to the front door. "Sorry, had a late meeting," she yelled as she tripped in the front door.

Andy was in the den, asleep on the couch, with the television on. The kids were all scattered in their rooms, doing who knows what. Dana went immediately into the kitchen, dropped her bags on one of the kitchen chairs and opened the refrigerator. Phew, she thought. *Glad I remembered to defrost something last night. I don't remember anything else.*

Dana pulled out the foil pan with home-made lasagna, mostly defrosted, and popped it in the oven. She went back to the refrigerator and grabbed everything she would need to make a salad, and placed it on the counter. She paused and listened. She heard nothing, so she quietly stepped over to the pantry, reached behind the row of cereal boxes, and found her emergency pint. Quickly, she opened it, threw her head back and took two gulps.

"Mom? Is that you?" She heard Matthew coming. Hurriedly, she put the cap back on and tossed the bottle on the floor of the pantry, behind all of the recyclable bags that had been collecting. Nobody will find it there, she thought.

"In the kitchen … starting dinner." She wiped her mouth as if that would cover the smell. Matthew had this amazing nose. He smelled things from another room.

"Do I smell Italian? I am soooo hungry"

"Geez, Matt! I just put it in the oven. You can't possibly smell it." This always amazed Dana, and it also kept her on her toes.

"Will it be ready soon? Dad and I have to leave pretty soon. The place is only open until nine and I know there's a lot of paperwork to do." Matthew came waltzing into the kitchen in shorts, a tee shirt and his socks. He hardly ever had shoes on. He liked to slide across the marble tile floors in the foyer.

"What are you talking about?" Dana tried to play dumb. She knew she should know what he was talking about, but she had no clue. She remembered nothing about the night before.

"The car, mom. We are supposed to pick up the car after dinner."

Dana spun around to face him, and put one of her silly faces on to show him that she was just fooling around, and said, "Car? What car?" She made a silly face. She figured if she could make a joke out of it, he wouldn't know she didn't remember. "Dinner will be ready in plenty of time. Are your sisters here?"

"Doing homework." Matthew reached into the bowl of salad vegetables that Dana had carefully been chopping to avoid making too much eye contact with him.

We spoke to Fernando on the phone last night, I remember that, she thought to herself. The dinner discussion had been that we had to get rid of the heap Matthew was driving because it was unsafe, and it was starting to cost real money to repair it. *I know I did some internet research. Hmmm,* she thought. *Wait. Andy did come back in the bedroom and tell me something about a car. Fernando was the guy who sold us our cars two weeks ago. What did Andy say?* This was killing her. She couldn't remember.

"Can we leave you with the dishes?" Andy asked. Andy used to help with the dishes every night. It was the few minutes out of each day that he and Dana had to talk, together, alone. No work, no kids, no television. This little bit of time was reserved for them. He had stopped that a while ago, the same way Dana had stopped bringing him his coffee to the bedroom in the mornings while he was getting ready for work. She remembered how she used to do it when they first started living together, when she had that old percolator.

"Go ahead." Dana was looking forward to them leaving. The other two kids would likely disappear into the den to watch TV or get on the computer. She could then go in the back and have an after dinner booster.

Something popped into her head, though. "*This is a progressive disease, and it gets worse, never better.*"

Before she finished her thought, they were gone.

CHAPTER 9

"Here's a perfect example of what I mean when I say I should have been born in the Victorian Era." Dana always smirks when she says this, but deep down in her heart, she really believed it. She was so uncomfortable with the "sexual revolution" and "free love." Images from Woodstock made her cringe, even though she loved the music. Open marriages, wife-swapping, and all of the themes of the sixties and seventies, while she was coming of age, were things that repulsed her. Dana was a prude. She evolved into that from her own life experiences and the way they made her feel.

"When I was going out with this guy I had known from high school during the summer before I went away to college, I was completely turned off. Not by him, but by his father." Dana sat forward on the edge of the couch in Carmen's office. She was a little light headed. She hadn't gotten herself completely smashed this particular night, but certainly she didn't want to let on to her therapist that she had been drinking even a little. Carmen had already been on her case about her drinking enough.

"I know," she continued. "I wasn't dating his father, I was dating Richie." She said it almost sarcastically, because those were actually Marge's words. She hated when her mother was right. "Richie had invited me to go with him and is family up to the Smokey Mountains for a weekend. I really wanted to go, because I love it up there. I love the hiking, the fishing and I wanted to see about going rafting."

"I told him, though, that I would go if I could have my own hotel room. I would pay for it myself." Dana was very smug and self-satisfied. "I didn't want him to think that because I was going away with him that he was going to have the time of his life ... or his dick would." Richie was kind of surprised, but agreed to the arrangements, because he really liked Dana.

"So, the first morning, casually over coffee, as if it was normal breakfast conversation, Richie's asshole dad pipes up with the fact that he thinks girls who don't put out by the second date aren't worth the third date." Dana slumped back into the couch, as if she had given up the battle. "It's always all about sex, isn't it?

"Did Richie say that? Carmen asked. "I mean, did he agree with his father?" Carmen was always trying to play devil's advocate. Sometimes it made Dana feel like she was always the one who was being interrogated or she was the one who was wrong in the circumstance.

"No, Geez!" Dana sat straight up. "He didn't defend my honor either, though, so my guess is he agreed with his father, the pig."

Carmen started to squirm. "I hate to do this, especially right now, but I need to run to the ladies' room. Hold that thought, and I'll be right back." She got up and headed for the door. Carmen, Dana found out later, had a bladder disorder. Guess she picked the wrong profession if she can't sit still for an hour, Dana thought to herself, maliciously.

Dana glanced around the small, moderately lit office. This lady liked flowers, had a Masters' degree, liked fine art, read a lot about her profession, and liked to play with blocks. There was a basket of toys in the corner, because Carmen had a few clients who were young enough that she engaged in play therapy. Dana yawned.

She leaned forward and listened. When she didn't hear the sound of footsteps, she decided to refresh herself. She reached into the bottom of her purse, which was perched precariously on the arm of the couch, and pulled out a half pint bottle of whiskey. There was just enough in it to do the trick, she thought. She quickly unscrewed the lid, put her lips to the top and threw her head back, gulping down three or four swigs. Without thinking anything of it, she screwed the lid back on and tossed the bottle in the small trash can next to the desk. The glass, while it didn't break, made a loud clanking noise just as the door opened.

"What was that?" Carmen asked as she closed the door behind her. "What was what?" Dana played dumb, but realized she had to find a way to get that bottle out of the trash. "I didn't hear anything." "Oh, okay. Now where were we?" Carmen sat back down in her desk chair, right next to the trash can. "Oh yeah, you were saying that

Richie agreed with his dad. How do you know that?"

"Okay, I don't really know." Dana was resigned to agree with whatever this lady said. She didn't want to rock the boat now, because she could already feel the liquor working on her. "I let him know how uncomfortable it made me feel, and soon thereafter, I stopped going out with him." She paused. "In a way, if he took it the right way, it probably helped him with future relationships … helping to keep his stupid father out of his business."

Dana didn't seem to notice, but she had begun slurring her words. Carmen cocked her head to the side. "Are you okay?" This was lip service only, because Carmen had already spotted the bottle out of the corner of her eye. She wanted to get Dana to admit it to her before she challenged her. "You seem a little groggy. Did you get enough sleep last night?"

"Enough of this shit." Dana stood up and grabbed her purse. "I'm fine. I think we've run out of time." She turned toward the door, but lost her balance. *I didn't have that much,* she thought to herself. Dana had forgotten that she had been nibbling on the Xanax during the day, too, so she was a little further gone than she had intended to be.

"Wait, you don't have to go. We were just scratching the surface here." Carmen didn't want her driving, and she always used that line when Dana would jump up to leave in a tirade. Carmen used the word florid to describe these outbursts, Dana would later find out.

"It's okay. I really don't feel like talking anymore anyway." Dana opened the door and was gone. She rode down the elevator lost in thought, wondering why she even did this. Another wasted session, another wasted evening. This lady is honestly trying to help her. The problem was that Dana hadn't yet reached the point where she wanted to help herself.

"Dana," Carmen lost Dana completely in her thoughts. "DANA!"

"Huh?" Dana shook her head.

"You really need to focus on curbing your drinking."

It reminded her of the night she had to block Dana's car in the parking lot. She had been so intoxicated, she actually left the session and went to buy more liquor, expecting to continue the session when she got back, Carmen recalled. Carmen had broken patient confidence back then by calling Andy to come get Dana to keep her from driving anymore. It saved her life then, but it may be too late this time. And poor Andy didn't catch on. He was clueless.

"Well I tried," Dana stated adamantly. "It's not for me."

"Tried what?" Carmen was rummaging through her briefcase looking for something that was obviously very important, and didn't seem to be focusing on Dana.

"I went to an AA meeting. Not for me."

"Okay, then." Carmen reached down to the bottom of the outer pouch of the leather briefcase and flung out her keys. "Phew! I thought I was going to have to cab it home tonight, and I hate those drivers."

"Okay then? That's it?

"I'm sorry, what did you say? I wasn't tuned in." Carmen was now settled in her desk chair, ready to work.

"What I said was I went to an AA meeting. It's not for me."

"Did you stay for the whole thing and really listen? You really can't base it on one meeting." Carmen tried to hold back her excitement at the prospect of this lady finally getting a hold of her addiction and fixing herself and her life. "Why don't you go to a different meeting if you didn't like that one?"

"I'll see."

"That's all I can ask." Carmen knew that pushing her wouldn't work. She had to find her own way. "Okay, so you wanted to talk about your Dad?"

"He was always so hard on me." Dana started. "I don't think he ever spontaneously told me he loved me, or that I was pretty or anything a little girl needs or wants to hear from her father." Dana leaned back against the couch, rested her head and stared at the ceiling. She didn't hate her father. Hate is such a strong word. She did, however, resent him.

"I did everything I could to please him, and it seems like it was never enough. I even wore my hair in a stupid style that he liked, because some movie star who he liked wore it that way. I went so far as to get my sixth grade picture with my hair tied in a ponytail to the side, over the left shoulder. I hated it. And he never said one word. Not one mention."

Carmen hesitantly interrupted here. What did you want him to do, or say?" She knew the answer, but she wanted Dana to own this. Dana kept her head back. She was uncomfortable making eye contact with this lady when she was talking about difficult things, and talking about her father was the most painful of all. She had always blamed most of her adult issues on the fact that her father created a monster in her. It was because of him that she was such a perfectionist. It was because of him that she was always looking for approval and acceptance. It was because of him that nothing she did was ever good enough in her mind. No matter how much people praised her, she always found a way to illuminate all the things that she had done wrong, or could have done better. She related the story of a colleague who knew immediately that her father had been hard on her, just by working with her only a few weeks.

"I wanted him to say I looked pretty without being prompted. I mean why did I have to be the one to say things like, Dad, how do I look?" Dana pouted like a child. "His stock answer would always be, 'okay, if you like that sort of thing.' I could have been Elizabeth Taylor, and it wouldn't have evoked any better a reaction."

Dana felt herself welling up with tears. She hated it when she cried over her father. She never cried when he passed away. She was too busy making sure her mother was okay, seeing to the business of things, and making sure she had everything she needed; listening to her grief and trying to be supportive. She gently wiped away the one tear that had escaped down the side of her face.

"Even when I worked with him, years ago, he was a tyrant. I mean, I'm glad I got the chance to learn the business from him, and it did give me a leg up to get the work experience, but every time I came in with a new contract, even if it was the most lucrative one we had ever secured, the best he could ever say to me was, 'what do you want from me … I expect that from you.'" She took a deep breath.

"Not good job or nice going." Another tear slipped out. "Just that he expected it of me."

Dana had gotten to the point where she really believed that's the way businesses were run. She didn't discover bonuses, thank you notes from bosses or vendors, employee of the month plaques or any of that stuff until her father retired and she went out into the real world. The problem, she felt, was that she took her father with her in her head, and was always on overdrive to perform. She worked too fast and too furious for her own good, always. She always created a high-stress environment for herself.

"Then there was the time I had been so fed up with the way he treated me, I got bold and daring." She sat up. Her right leg was bouncing uncontrollably as she continued. "He was always preaching about how we had to separate work and family. He wanted me to train somebody to cover for me while I was out to deliver Matthew, my oldest. When I tried to tell him the girl wasn't getting it, he didn't listen. When I went to do payroll, I saw that he was paying her considerably more than me."

Now Dana was wringing her hands again, in that familiar circular motion. "When I challenged him on that, he told me it was because that was her only source of income, and that I at least could rely on Andy's income. I told him that's not the way things are done in business. Didn't she have to earn it? She had no clue what she's doing, even after I had shown her four or five times. His answer to me was that 'what he pays her is none of my business.'"

Dana began to breathe harder and the tears were starting to come steadily. "Carmen, I once asked him if he even loved me, and do you know what his answer was?"

Carmen was very still. She was, in essence, afraid to ask for the answer. She knew they were in a very raw part of Dana's past, and working through this would ultimately be a good thing, but she also knew that when Dana had really tough sessions, she also went home and numbed herself. Carmen knew she was still drinking, although she appeared to be sober tonight. "What did he say?"

"Well, there's a question." Dana broke into convulsive tears. "And it wasn't well, now *THERE'S* a question. It was, now there's a QUESTION." I know those words can be misconstrued, but if you were there, you would have understood his meaning." Dana cried through the next convulsion. It was almost as if she was in labor, working through each contraction. She rubbed her nose with her arm. "My father had a habit of playing mind games with my emotions." She took a deep breath, and then collapsed back into the couch, and reached for a tissue.

"That was the day I quit working for him. I had to. Matthew was due any day, and I couldn't deal with the stress anymore. I wanted to be able to relax and be calm when delivery finally came." A small smile began to replace the pained expression on Dana's face. That always happened when she talked about her kids... all three of them, even though she has trouble relating to the girls, because they're so girly. She absolutely loved her role as mom, having difficulty with the fact that Matt would be leaving for school in the fall, and the girls would only be home another two years.

"It was almost like a victory for me when he came back to me, kind of with his tail between his legs, when Matthew was about three months old." Dana was smug, although it didn't become her. "I really had to hold my tongue and not be all 'I told you so' when he almost begged me to come back to the studio and work for him again." Dana was trying not to sound bitchy, but it was coming through.

"He actually admitted to me that I was right about that bimbo. He had to fire her because she was making so many mistakes." She snickered, just a little. "She actually sent the wrong script to a very touchy talent. She sent the supporting role script to a star, by courier, no less. Imagine that!" Now she was laughing out loud. "I wish I could have seen Dad's face when he got that phone call!"

Carmen was intrigued. "So, did you go back?"

"Of course I did. But it was on my terms. I got to take Matt with me, and I got a raise and a new title. He was going to pay me at least what he was paying that dumb shit, or I wouldn't even consider it." Dana sighed. "But it didn't last too long. Dad had a heart attack a few months later, and decided to sell the business. I didn't have the capital to buy it, nor did I want the total responsibility, so I went on unemployment, and he retired."

"That's when I got into the marketing gig. And that was an accident. But I'll take it, since it's been a good fit, so far." Dana grinned. "And it's one thing about which my father can't tell me what to do and how to do it, because he has no earthly idea what I'm talking about." She paused. "But then, that never stopped him before. Anytime I had to talk to him about anything, he was usually busy trying to think of what he was going to say next rather than listening to me."

Carmen took a deep breath. She was seeing the pattern. "That was a lot to unfold. You okay?"

"I feel like I've been hit by a bus," Dana answered.

"Let's pick up with this next week, unless there's something that gets in the way of that." Carmen rolled her chair over to her desk and opened her appointment book. "Already have you down. Things going okay at home?"

"No, but it doesn't matter."

"Dana, it does matter. I really don't like it when you say things like that." Carmen has been very patient with this florid and dramatic woman. "We'll get to work on that too. How about the drinking?"

"Know what? That doesn't matter either." Dana stood up defiantly, grabbed her bag and headed for the door.

"Please don't leave like this." Carmen stood up. She was determined not to chase her down. "I really wish you would not leave like this."

She was gone.

"Don't you have any nice memories about your father?"

"Geez, you sound like my mother." Dana slumped back down into the couch. Ever since Dad died it seemed her mother had forgotten how brutal he had been at times, even to her. Even towards the end, Dad had gone so far as to get physical, and poor mom had basically blocked that out of her memory. Dana figured that was a defense mechanism, and wasn't about to upset her mother with it.

Dana had anticipated having an upbeat session with Carmen tonight. She was tired of dragging herself home back to Andy every week and having him ask how it went. She always had one of two answers, depending on her state of mind. One was 'none of your business,' if she was in a particularly aggressive mood, and the other was that she 'felt like a dishrag,' if they had worked on something intense.

"My dad didn't really leave much room for a lot of good memories. I mean, we did hang out around the piano together, to play and sing. That was nice." She tried to hold on to those memories, especially when she was trying to fend off her anger at him, both for being so hard on her and also for dying so young. "We used to sing a lot of show music together."

"What I seem to remember more when I was a kid is the fact that he was the punisher. You know the old 'wait till your father gets home' threat from my mother. I had one, count 'em, one bad report card. In fact, it happened to be a very good report card with one bad grade. I got a D in algebra ONE semester. I just couldn't catch on. He made me quit the hockey team until I brought the grade up. Never mind that the rest of the grades were all A's and one B." The furrow in Dana's brow was deep. Carmen recognized this expression. It usually meant there was more anger coming.

"He never was able to make it to any of my plays or my games. The one and only time he made it to a basketball game, he called me hot dog because I was trying too hard to impress him." Dana drew silent for a moment. "That was the night I ran away from home." Dana's face relaxed just enough so that Carmen could detect a sinister grin. "I hid in the basement for four hours. Jerks. They never thought to look there. Had the police out looking for me. It was snowing and bitter cold."

Carmen rolled her eyes. Unfortunately, Dana saw this. "What?" Her anger swelled.

"That was a cruel thing to do," Carmen started.

Dana cut her off. "Tough shit," she asserted. She paused. Her memory made her feel very small, all of a sudden. She lost her forcefulness and her confidence. "As it turns out, I caved."

"How do you mean?" Carmen was very curious now.

"Once again, I took the blame for all of it. Told him he was right. I said I was wrong for running, a spoiled brat. They give me too much … He had me decide my own punishment. And, once again, I was extremely hard on myself." She was shaking her head. She knew then and she knew now that it had been a cruel thing to do, but she was really hurt. Just once she had wanted him to engage in her life in a good way, and not have it end ugly.

"Dad let me be. He never took any responsibility in any of what happened that night. He would NEVER admit he was wrong about anything."

"We even had a standing joke about it later on. We were having dinner with a friend of his who was a math whiz, and could figure out exactly how many days old you were, in seconds of hearing your birth date. When he did mine, he wrote down the number. Dad and I both guessed. I was right and Dad was wrong, and the only thing he could say was, 'Eat your soup.' To this day, even though he's been gone over 10 years, whenever anyone in the family is proven to be in error, we say 'eat your soup.'"

"I think the worst part of all of it is that he never made me feel good about myself. He only pointed out my short-comings." Dana started to tear up, again. Maybe this is how I grieve for him, she thought. Maybe this is the way I'll get over his death once and for all.

"I watched so many friends with their dads when I was growing up. To be fair, it was a different age. Still, so many of them seemed kinder and more approachable." Dana remembered sleepovers at friends' houses and birthday parties. She remembered being invited to stay for dinner at someone's house. Their families were somehow different. Their dads would ask her questions and actually listen to the answers. She was jealous of the relationships so many of her friends had with their dads.

Carmen inadvertently let out a deep sigh. Being extremely aware of other people's reactions and opinions of her, Dana jumped on the defensive.

"What's wrong? Did I say something wrong?"

"Not at all." Carmen, in her attempt to reassure her client, made things worse. "I just feel bad that you felt that way."

The spigot burst. Dana's self-control went out the window. She wasn't sure why it was happening right at that moment. She wondered, maybe, if it was because she finally felt as if someone heard her; someone was giving her a voice. "I swear, just once, if he could have told me I was good or I was pretty. It was always a fucking game to him."

"Maybe he didn't know how."

"He always used that as an excuse. He always told me he had a 'not so normal' upbringing because he lost his mother early, and his dad wasn't around much." Dana reached for a tissue, but the box was empty. She rifled through her purse and found an empty package. By the time she looked up, Carmen had found one in her purse. "That doesn't change what it did to me."

Dana drew a long breath and let it out slowly. "I guess he did the best he could. He seemed to have no problem relating to all of his grandchildren." Dana blew her nose gently. "What was so difficult about doing the same thing with his own kids? I have two brothers that feel the exact same way as I do. We're all fucked up in one way or another."

"Grandchildren are different. You know that."

"I remember once when we had a talk. He actually stopped talking long enough to hear what I had to say." Dana tried to leave her sarcasm aside. "We talked about just that. I said to him, 'Dad, you know it isn't too late.'"

"Too late for what," asked Carmen?

"It isn't too late to salvage and rebuild a relationship with your own kids. You just have to be present … available. That's all." Dana was ready to rattle off the times he wasn't present. He missed her high school graduation, her college graduation, she had already told her about all of her plays and games. When she had her second miscarriage, Dana was only three miles from his office, and he couldn't even take the time to see her in the hospital. He was never there when it counted. Why are men so insensitive? He had used the excuse that he had work to do, and that he'd be there later. He never managed to get there. Dana tried hard to accept her mother's explanation that her father got squirrely around hospitals because of his mother's illness and that he had always been that way around sick people. "I guess I need to learn to forgive him a little."

"I often think about his funeral. There must have been over four hundred people there. Four hundred people who knew and loved him, and I didn't know who hardly any of them were. He was obviously present in their lives."

Dana sat back against the headrest of the couch and stared at the ceiling through her bloodshot eyes. This time, they were red from crying, not from drinking. "I do have to admit, that despite all of the other issues I'm having with him, my husband is an amazing father." Dana rarely gives Andy credit for anything during a session, so Carmen was surprised by this. "Andy NEVER misses a game or a school function. He always checks on the kids when their sick, helps with homework, helps with birthday parties. He wouldn't miss any of it for anything." She almost smiled. "I kind of knew this about him when I met his Dad. Andy's dad would just light up when any of his kids walked into the room. My dad would barely notice."

Carmen glanced at the clock. She is always astounded at how fast the time goes when she works with Dana. "Dana we really need to wrap this up. I do have a question," she said as she rolled over to her desk. "Do you ever tell Andy how much you appreciate his parenting?"

"Absolutely. It's the one last bastion of common ground we have right now. I'm holding on to it for dear life."

"I don't even know what to do. He's hiding money from me. I don't know if he's getting ready to divorce me, or he's doing something illegal or what?" Dana was hysterical on the phone to Carmen. "Do I confront him? What should I say? Oh my God I can't breathe."

"You can breathe." Carmen started. "Don't jump to any conclusions here." Carmen had no idea what to say to this woman. Her husband had a hidden bank account with thousands of dollars tucked away. It could be any number of things, but to surmise anything could create even more problems than already existed.

"Dana." Carmen heard nothing. "Are you still there?" There was silence, and then a sudden gasp.

"How can I ever trust him again? Maybe the marriage really is over. Is he doing something illegal? Is there another woman he's keeping? Is this why he's bringing so little pay home? What the fuck is he doing?" Dana was trembling with each new possibility.

"I want you to go home and take a warm shower. DO NOT DRINK anything. You need to be clear-headed when you confront him." She paused, and then added, "And you will have to confront him." Carmen decided that the best approach would be a direct one. She knew from her few sessions with Andy that he would not be able to lie to Dana about this, so the truth would come out almost immediately.

"Will you be available later?" Dana was visibly shaken. "Can I call you if I get into trouble?"

"I have other people through about 8:30, but I'll keep my phone available after that," Carmen answered.

Dana had found a bank deposit slip of an account she didn't recognize, and since she kept the family finances, she was clearly curious. She called the bank and used Andy's social security number and the same password he uses for everything, easily discovering the account.

None of his explanations made sense to Dana. Nothing he said was good enough to calm her. She didn't believe a word he said. She stood frozen, in a state of horror, her pulse throbbing in her neck. Trying to process what he was saying Dana only felt the pounding in her head, her tongue sticking to the roof of her mouth.

"It was bonus money." Andy hung his head. "I didn't do anything illegal or immoral."

"Hiding thousands of dollars from your family isn't immoral? A bonus? Why didn't you tell me?" Dana tried as hard as she could to maintain her composure but her emotions were overtaking any sense of calm. "I've been going around in stained old clothes that are four sizes too big for me, using safety pins to hold them on, because we didn't have money." Her rage was now palpable. "I can't tell you how many times I've had to say no to your children because we couldn't afford it." She was nearly winded. "We've been on the tightest of food budgets. I've been buying lower quality meats and produce to cut corners and it's been breaking my heart. If I serve one more hot dog we're all going to get cancer."

"I'm embarrassed to tell you."

"Bullshit." Dana was just plain angry now. "I'm your wife for God's sake. We're supposed to be able to tell each other anything."

Andy had been depositing his paychecks in that secret account and writing himself bigger ones to deposit in their joint account so it would look like he was earning more that he actually was. His ego had overtaken him, and he was ashamed of the fact that he couldn't support his family better.

"Not a good reason to lie to me."

"You have been lying about your drinking." Andy was sure that by going on the offensive he could deflect Dana.

"Not true. I never lied about my drinking. You're the one who was offering me a drink every fucking night. I just didn't mention that I had already had a few." Dana's fury was rising.

"Same thing."

"No it's not. You forced your family to live without things we needed when we could have had them."

"Yeah, well you forced your family to live without … you … their mother."

"Bastard." She knew he was right. "Bitch." He knew she had a point. "Get out."

"I'm not going anywhere."

Dana must have left four messages on Carmen's voice mail. She was locked in the bedroom after asking or yelling at Andy to leave. He wouldn't. She didn't have a bottle back there. It was time to face things with a clear head. Andy could be so cruel, in fact reprehensible when he was angry.

Carmen finally called back. Dana told him as much as she could remember, but her account was extremely emotional, and therefore probably not completely accurate. She always accused Andy of embellishing a story, but she was good at it as well, especially when it was laced with anger.

"I'll call Andy in the morning." Carmen attempted to diffuse the situation. "I think he should see a male therapist to deal with some of these issues. We can work together on the marriage, still, and you and I can continue separately."

Matthew found Dana outside on the patio, fiddling with her plants. He noticed her hands were shaking as she tried to pick up a tiny seed from a bowl to slip it carefully into a peat pot for the greenhouse vegetable garden on which she was working.

"Mom, are you okay?" He was pretty sure he knew what was happening. Matthew had noticed the smell of liquor on her breath often, and was pretty sure she was doing a lot of heavy drinking. Sometimes he cursed that nose of his. He was scared to death to say anything, so he didn't. He was going back to school in two days anyway, and besides, there was nothing he was going to be able to do to change anything.

"Sure," said Dana. "These seeds are just so damn tiny. I can't get … wait … Oh Shit." Dana looked up at Matthew. She knew he knew. She couldn't make eye contact. Only excuses. "Oops."

"I'm going over to the high school to shoot some hoops. I'll be back in a few hours." Matthew knew that was just a way to get out and that he wouldn't be back until right before dinner.

"Where are your sisters?" Dana asked innocently.

"Mom … don't you remember? They're over at Nana's. You took them over last night to sleep over." Dana was kicking herself. She vaguely remembered driving them over, but can't recall anything after that. How did she get home? Where was Andy during all of this? How much did she drink anyway? God, what was she doing driving the kids?

Dana was at that same AA room at 7:00 the next morning. This time she meant business. Whatever it took, she was going to get a handle on this. She swore to herself she would never drive a car, especially with her children in it, under the influence of alcohol, again.

"You do realize that nothing you've said in the rooms of Alcoholics Anonymous is that big of a deal," began Dana's sponsor. "We've all done what we think are horrible things, only to find out that once we've shared them, they don't seem so horrible. Somebody else has already 'been there, done that." Lisa didn't take any crap from Dana, and was teaching her honesty, love and tolerance, gratitude and most of all, acceptance. "A burden shared is half, and all that shit."

"I guess if I'm going to get this I have to come completely clean." Dana began to unfold the rest of her story to Lisa, much as she had to her therapist...

CHAPTER 10

"I really think if he knew about my past he would be totally turned off." Dana spoke defiantly. There was no way in hell she was going to tell him about Michelle, the near-rape, the abuse. *He gets squeamish just talking about homosexuality, incensed about rape, and my God, what would he do if he knew I was taken advantage of by my own relative*, she thought.

Carmen understood that for the most part, but she didn't think Andy was the big bad ogre of whom Dana was painting this picture. She saw Andy as a relatively simple man, who didn't think as much about things as his wife did. He just wanted things to be calm again, and he just wanted to feel close to Dana again. *Oh, who was she kidding? He just wanted to get laid once in a while.*

"Dana, Andy loves you to his very core. He is a lot more forgiving than you think and he is not as inflexible. He just has an issue with anger."

"Damn straight he does. I'm scared to death of his acid tongue." Dana slumped down into the couch. Ever since she had started regular therapy with Carmen, so much has happened. Besides the fact that this wacky woman was the only one to ever see through her and thereby get her to take positive steps toward stopping the drinking, Carmen was also able to get Dana to really talk about things that had been buried so deep she had forgotten they were there. Only now is she starting to see how so much of it shaped who she is and how she approaches so many things in her life ... especially men, marriage and sex.

"The worst things come out his mouth when he's mad." Dana rested her head back and stared at the ceiling. "He tried to threaten to divorce me, sue me for custody of the kids and then leave me with the pathetic group health insurance I get at work." She reflected back on his exact words. "You'll sit in waiting rooms for hours, waiting to see lousy doctors who give sub-par care, just to reach their quotas. None of your precious doctors will be on those plans."

"All I could think of was those were the two meanest things he could do," Dana continued. "My children are my life, and my health teeters anyway. I can't change some of the doctors who have been taking care of my case for years." Tiny droplets began to run down the sides of Danas face and into her ears. She sat up wiping them away. "I thought he was just so fucking cruel. I was saying the meanest thing I could think of, then." She took a long, deep breath. "I told him I hoped I would drop dead right in front of him."

"Ouch!" Carmen leaned forward and handed her a tissue. "Guess he has no corner on the market when it comes to acid tongues." Carmen waited for some kind of acknowledgement, but got none. "So let's talk about these issues ... these things that you are so afraid to tell him."

"First of all," Dana started. "With my new found sobriety, I have tendency to be so brutally honest, that I am afraid I'm going to say things that really hurt him. You know, the things that are about him." Dana sat forward on the edge of the couch, and began to wring her hands in a rhythmic motion, around and around.

"I really don't know where to start. I mean, he knows all about my relationship with my Dad. He knows I've always had self-esteem problems and feelings of low self-worth." She cracked a small smile. "Funny thing is, he never understood why. Andy's always telling me that he's my biggest fan." The smile went away. "He also doesn't understand, though, why things that happened so many years ago still affect me so intensely. He says things like 'that happened 45 years ago, isn't it time to forget about it?'"

Dana sat, pensively, and then added, "Funny, how he can say that to me, but can't see it in himself ... about the money stuff ..."

CHAPTER 11

"Why do men equate love with sex?" Dana couldn't figure it out. She showed Andy a thousand different ways in which she loves him. She just didn't have any interest in sex. Her desire was gone. She had no libido, which did concern her a little. It isn't like she was looking for it somewhere else. She had basically stopped looking for sex anywhere … at home, in men, in women. She just had no interest. She had even lost interest in pleasuring herself.

"He thinks that just because I won't fuck him, that I don't love him." Dana sat with her arms crossed on the edge of the couch, bouncing her one knee, and pinching the insides of her arms. She wasn't sure if she was angry at him or anxious, disappointed in him or depressed. She just knew that their marriage was faltering because of this issue. She truly believes that if she would have sex with him, he would think everything is okay. And it wasn't.

"I think it's time for us to work on this together. All three of us," said Carmen. "He needs to know how you feel." She sat back in her desk chair, and because it was on a swivel, she lost her balance a little.

"First, he needs to know where you are in your life physically; that women when they go through the change have less energy, and less estrogen. He also needs to understand that some of your medications are working against your libido, so you have a double whammy." She paused for a minute. "And Dana, while you can't really come forward with a lot of what we've talked about, you do know that part of your issues stem from that, right?"

"He knows about college. I don't think he ever really took it seriously." She thought for a minute. "I only remember way back when we were dating, going to the movies with him to see 'Victor, Victoria,' and how squeamish he was even thinking about homosexuality. I used to tease him about how the people most vocal against it, are usually the ones most afraid that it lives within them."

"He never actually agreed with me when I would say things like 'I think everyone has the potential of loving anyone in anyway.'" Dana used to use that as her validation and justification for having had that relationship with Michelle. She thought about it all the time. When Dana had first told Carmen about it, it had been the first time she had verbalized anything about it in over twenty years. She was overwhelmed by it, and felt so exposed for having done so, that she swore to herself she would never speak of it again, but what happened was the opposite. She found herself floundering in panic attacks, one right after the other. She actually had to call Carmen and tell her that she was panicking. Carmen had to assuage her fear by reminding her of her own oath of patient confidentiality … convincing Dana that she would never tell anyone anything that was shared in her office.

Dana found that by telling Carmen about this piece of her most complicated puzzle, she it would only I lead to herself questioning her own sexuality so much deeper. She started looking at women differently, and even flirting with some of them whom she knew were gay or bisexual. Her sexual fantasies became about women, and even when she was having sex with Andy, she was only able to become completely aroused by memories of Michelle. She questioned whether marrying a man was just another one of those decisions she made because it was what she was supposed to do. Was she living a lie? Was she supposed to have lived a totally different life?

She even fell into the grateful patient trap and had a crush on Carmen, for God's sakes. Dana constantly found herself trying to catch a glimpse of Carmen when she wasn't looking. It didn't start out to be sexual in nature, but she found herself getting unusually aroused just sitting in the same room with her. She began to fantasize when she was away, although she already knew nothing would ever happen. When she got up the nerve to tell her, Carmen put out that fire immediately. With her sense of humor, though, Dana loved to tease Carmen about it. Whenever there was any suggestive opportunity, Dana would take it, with a smirk on her face, looking forward to Carmen's reaction.

"So," Carmen began, "When do you think the man-bashing really started?"

"It's really hard to talk about this." Dana looked away from her therapist. "I've never told anybody about this, but having relived this episode of what, today, would be referred to as sexual abuse, over and over in her mind and even though it happened forty-five years ago, she was all of a sudden having flashbacks. At six years old, she didn't even know, at the time, they were sex acts and that it was wrong.

"Wrap your fingers around it a little tighter," he said. Dana opened her grip and curled her little fingers around again. "Good, now do it a little faster." Dana sat on the side the bed, following instructions. After all, there was a Milky Way in it for her.

"Faster!" Gary turned slightly on his side toward Dana. "Faster." He started to thrust his hips up and down but that ruined the rhythm. He fell back down on the bed. "Keep going … Faster … "

Dana had no idea what was happening. All she knew was that Gary had locked his bedroom door after he offered her a candy bar. She loved Milky Way candy bars, and Gary always had a stash. He was lying on his bed with his pants pulled down to his hips and his thing was sticking out. Dana had never seen one. Even with all the boys that came and went from the house, she had never seen any of them naked, unless it was when she was a baby and they were bathed together. Here she was, six years old and getting a close up view.

Gary arched his back and moaned. "Here it is. Here it is." She let go of her clenched fist and lurched away.

"EEWWWWW." She squealed. "What is that?

"It's nothing, shhhhhh." Gary didn't want anyone hearing her. "Well, eewwww. It's sticky." She wiped her hand on the blanket

next to her. "I don't like it." She stood up indignantly, and put her handout. "Where's my candy."

Gary was pleased with the outcome of this endeavor, so he had no problem fulfilling his part of the deal. He reached over and opened the drawer of his bedside table and said, "Help yourself." He fell back onto the bed and added, "Now get out of my room."

Dana grabbed the candy bar, and bolted for the door. Her next idea was to go wash the hair of her Thumbelina doll.

Gary wiped himself off, and then started the process all over again, this time on his own. This is what thirteen year-old-boys do.

Dana remembered out loud how it was that she discovered that what happened with Gary was wrong. "I had been away at sleepover camp and was in arts and crafts one day." She tried to avoid making eye contact with her therapist. She had been seeing this lady for a few years already. She knew more about Dana then Dana knew herself. Was she embarrassed yet again?

She thought back to the time she admitted to Carmen about her relationship with Michelle. Carmen didn't bat an eye while Dana went off into a raging journey of disgrace, anxiety and panic. She had exposed herself. She had revealed her deepest, darkest secret. And even if Carmen was, by law, not allowed to share anything they discussed, she still felt vulnerable.

"Dana! You're doing great." Carmen always encouraged her to try to stay on course. Dana's mind never could stay in one place very long. She often talked about three things in the same sentence, for God's sake.

"Oh, yeah …" Dana took a deep breath. "Oh right, I was at camp, and I was drawing a picture of a man with an erect penis. Pretty nice detail, if you ask me." A pained expression came over her face and she started to breathe slightly faster. "The counselor's name was Doreen. I'll never forget it. I even remember what she was wearing."

Dana sat upright on the couch. "She snatched the picture from me and glared at me as if I had done something absolutely horrific." Dana gasped as if she had stopped breathing for a minute. "She took it and quickly left the building, heading across to the camp office." Dana paused. "I knew I was in trouble, but I wasn't really sure why."

Carmen interrupted. "And now, you know that what happened to you was wrong, and kind of creepy." She tried to come across in a matter-of-fact way, but after working with Dana for so long, she knew that this was just one small piece of how Dana developed her attitude about men, about sex, about herself and about life in general. Carmen wanted to assure Dana that she wasn't a pariah … that everyone has a past that contains things that might be upsetting. She couldn't find a good place to interject even the slightest encouragement.

"It wasn't until I connected the picture and the counselor's reaction, several months later, that a six-year-old little girl shouldn't have such a clear understanding of the anatomy of a male, and certainly not of an erect penis. Only then did I figure out that it was wrong and it was dirty and it was creepy."

Dana began to weep. "It didn't happen again, but it stayed with me. Several years later, when we were packing up to move to Atlanta, I found the picture in the attic. My mom had asked me to go up there and grab anything I wanted to take because the rest was getting thrown out, donated or sold at the yard sale."

Dana stared at the ceiling. "I can't believe my parents knew I drew that picture. Someone had written the date and a comment on it, I'm guessing the Camp Director, which said, "Don't you wish you were hung like this?" She sighed. At twelve, Dana had figured out that this was a sarcastic and suggestive reference because by then, she knew a lot more about anatomy, sex, and men. What she couldn't handle was that her parents knew she could draw a naked man at age six. "If only they had known what precipitated the drawingthat anatomically correct drawingmaybe they could have done something to help me …"

Dana's weeping had grown proportionately with the intensity of her story. She was now crying convulsively. "I remember tearing up the picture into tiny little pieces, and throwing part of it in three different trash cans around the house, assuring myself that they wouldn't end up together ever again." *Except in my mind.*

Finally, Carmen found the opportunity. "You do realize that while this is a little unusual, it isn't the end of the world." Carmen had worked as a sex therapist for many years and was beginning to see that between her new found sobriety and her fixation on some of these events from her childhood, Dana was having difficulty opening up to her husband not only about all of these things, but as a result, in a physical way either. The intimacy of this union had no chance if left to their own devices.

"I'd like for you and Andy to try something. It's something that may help bring back some of the openness and closeness you once had." Carmen rolled her chair across the floor and began rooting through her file cabinet, eventually pulling a folder out of the bottom drawer. She rifled through the file of papers, pulling out a few pages. "I'm going to give you some exercises in something called Sensate Focus. Read this through, and I want you to try just Part One, and then let's talk next week." She handed the papers to Dana. "I mean with Andy. I mean bring Andy with you. I mean, do the exercises AND bring Andy next week."

"Nothing happened." Dana sat stoically with her arms crossed on the couch. "I couldn't even bring myself to tell him about this junk." She had stuffed the paperwork Carmen had given the previous week down into the bottom of her purse.

"That's okay. It'll be there when you're ready." If Carmen had learned nothing else about Dana, it was that this is a woman who could not be pushed. She didn't do anything until she was ready. "We can pick up where we left off last week, if you want."

"Nothing more to say about that. I mean, it never happened again, but it did stay in my head." Dana never let go of things that she felt harms her. It's almost as if she derived some sort of sick pleasure from reliving painful memories. She decided to tell Carmen some more stories about why she had issues with men and sex.

She got comfortable on the couch and staring at the ceiling, launched into another narrative ...

Dave's party looked like it was going to be a bust. It's hard for teenagers to be quiet in a small apartment complex and still have fun. The neighbor upstairs had them turn down the music; the neighbor next door threatened to call the police if they didn't stop screaming.

"Let's just move it over to my place!" Hope lived with her parents in a large home in Marietta, and they had an indoor swimming pool. "My parents aren't home. Who needs a ride?"

Everybody car-pooled over. Dana was reluctant to go, because she knew this was a fast and furious crowd. They reminded her of her days back in Vermont when she got herself caught up with the "popular" kids for all the wrong reasons.

At Hope's house, everyone was sitting around the pool, talking and laughing. Dana sat on the outside edge of the group, contributing very little. Hope asked if anyone wanted to swim. "I didn't bring a bathing suit," Dana said innocently.

"Don't need one." Hope crossed her arms down, grabbed the bottom of her shirt and pulled it up over her head. She dropped the shirt on the floor and then reached around the back with her right hand and quickly unsnapped her bra, revealing perfectly shaped, unblemished, and firm 16-year-old breasts. Everyone stared, including Dana.

Two boys jumped up, pulled off their shirts and dropped their pants, leaving on their underwear. Dave turned to Dana. "Come with me." He took her by the hand and led her to the cabana changing room. Dana had been suffering a wild crush on Dave for two years. Now was her moment.

He closed the door behind him. "Are you going to skinny dip?" "Are you?"

"Yep. Looks like fun." He took off his tee-shirt the same way Hope had, grabbed a towel from the shelf and wrapped it around his waist. He then reached underneath and removed his jeans and underwear, kicking off his sneakers and socks at the same time.

Dave stood there waiting for Dana to do something. All she could do was stare at the towel, and in so doing, make Dave somewhat self-conscious of his erection. She wasn't self-conscious, she was terrified. "I don't think I'm going to swim." She searched for an excuse. "I'm getting over bronchitis. Don't wanna mess with that. I just finished the antibiotic today." The last thing she wanted to do was fall into the same trap of doing something promiscuous, especially if she didn't want to, just to fit in, or to get a boyfriend.

"Okay, suit yourself." He started out of the cabana and then turned around. "Hey, I made pun."

Dana was one of only two people who chose not to join in. The other was this girl named Judy, who had a reputation for being a goodytwo shoes. In fact, they all called her "Jude the Prude." Dana was extremely uncomfortable. She got up and found her way to the kitchen, called home and got her brother Max. Max was a little high, but agreedto come pick her up. She decided to wait out front.

I guess a relationship with Dave isn't going to happen, she thought to herself. Hey, I madea pun at least I went to the party. That'll keep my mother quiet for a little while anyway. She could feel the tears coming up, but she didn't want to let them out. She didn't want to have to get into adiscussion with Max. He was always trying to give her advice aboutboys. Easy for him. He was popular.

"Carmen, why did I always find myself asking herself the same question after every party or social encounter? Why did I hate those things so much? What did I have to do to make friends? How far did I have to go?"

"Home in bed that night, I remember just lying there on my back, staring at the light pattern on the ceiling that snaked in from behind the window shades. I remember, feeling the tiny tears slither down my face and onto my pillow, next to my ear. Why did I always feel so empty?"

Dana started to weep again. "Why do I still, to this day, always feel so empty?" Dana put her head back on the head rest of the couch, and looking toward the ceiling, closed her eyes.

Her "tween" years were spent doing whatever she could do to make and keep friends. When everyone was naturally beginning to show interest in the opposite sex, so was she. Or at least she thought.

She wanted nothing more than to fit in, and she was somehow being accepted by the popular group who had a club called the "Punks, Patriots and Pussies," because they were all athletic, and the presumption was that they were a "fast crowd." At the time, she thought pussies referred to kitty cats. She didn't get it then.

Dana really didn't want to do some of the things they were doing. She laid on her back, having been tackled by Jimmy, the club's leader. He was straddling her hips and fighting with her to pull her shirt up. There they were, right in the foyer of his house, by the front door. Everyone was standing around laughing at them. Dana didn't think it was funny. She hated the whole situation. She hated Jimmy and she hated the club. Unexpectedly, Jimmy's mother came out of the kitchen and down the hall towards them, wiping her hands on a kitchen towel. "James, get up." She snapped at him. "That's not nice." Reluctantly, Jimmy rolled off of Dana and she got up, trying to put herself together.

Jimmy was not happy, so she was kicked out of the club.

Dana tried everything to get back in, including several episodes of exposing herself to the boys at school in a very public way. Dana had stood in the closet behind the teacher's desk, lifted her dress, dropping her underwear and whispered for them to look. She didn't know who saw. She didn't even know why she did it. She was desperate to get back in with the cool kids, but it never happened. All that was left was the shame she felt for doing what she did, and, of course, the ridicule that came with it. She had really begun to hate Vermont. She was actually happy to move away. It was turning out, though, that Atlanta wasn't much better for her.

"It's 11:00 on a school night. Tell him to go home." Marge yelled from the back bedroom.

"It's just Howard, Mom." Dana opened the door and let Howard in. Howard was on the tennis team with her brother, Max, but he was in Dana's class. He was just a friend, and the 'little sister' covenant was obviously in play here, because they would never be anything more than just friends.

"Want some pizza? I was hungry and I hate to eat alone!" Howard brushed past Dana and headed for her bedroom.

"Not allowed to have you in there." Dana rolled her eyes. It was a stupid rule. If her parents knew anything about her, they would know it was a stupid rule. "Dining room."

Howard danced around and circled back through the living room, almost losing his grip on the pizza, but landing it ever so gently on the end of the table.

"My mom doesn't know that tomorrow is a teacher's planning day. She thinks there's school tomorrow. I'll be right back." Dana disappeared in the back for a minute while Howard dove into the pizza. "Got that straightened out." Dana sat at the table opposite her friend. Howard was always a good sounding board about school and parents problems, but she didn't think she could talk to him about guys. So since there was nothing much more to talk about, they ate in silence for a little while.

"Need to run something by you." Howard said, seriously. He couldn't seem to start, as if he had either forgotten what he was going to say, or that he changed his mind.

"What is it?" Dana said with her mouth full.

"Promise you won't say anything?"

"Not if you don't want me to."

"Okay, well …" He paused again. Howard took a huge bite of pizza. Now, with a full mouth, he could gather himself and still change his mind. *"You know what? Never mind. Now's not the time."*

"Whatever you want." She shrugged her shoulders. This was nothing new from him. He always had great gossip, but tried hard not to be one. *"Wanna play some Pong?"*

"No, not really." He finished off his third piece and stood up. *"Do you want anymore? I promised my sister a piece or two."*

"Take it."

And as fast as he arrived, he was gone. That was the problem. There were very few people Dana felt comfortable around, Howard being one of them, but none of them were ever really around. They all had lives.

"Where's Howard?" Marge asked as she scuffed through the kitchen. *"Gone already?"* Marge loved to be around all the kids' friends. She always told Dana it made her feel young. And Dana, of course, would roll her eyes back into her head, responding with some rude or disrespectful comeback. She wouldn't go as far as saying she hated her mother, but she definitely hated how nosy she was.

"Then there was the Junior Prom. I ended up going with someone that didn't go to my school." Dana was telling this story to Carmen in a matter-of-fact way. She didn't feel like being in a therapy session. She would have rather been drinking tonight, she thought.

Carmen sat back in her chair, and dabbed her eyes with a tissue. She was fighting a cold and didn't feel like being at work. "Go on."

"You know, you're not really my cousin," I had to tell him," she continued. "Your father is cousins with my grandfather's second wife. We're not related by blood. It's okay to like me." Dana just shook her head. She had tried to make Steve understand that he wasn't doing something perverted by taking her to the Junior Prom. "I didn't want to be there in the first place."

"It was my mother's idea. I should have stopped the whole thing right then and there. 'Marge's ideas' are the two words that would send me into a spasm. I hated shopping for the outfit. I hated mom messing with my hair. I hated her for forcing me to put on just a hint of makeup. And then asking embarrassing questions like, "Did you put on deodorant?" Dana flopped back on the familiar couch and stared at the ceiling.

"So Dana was going to the Junior Prom with her cousin." Carmen repeated this out loud. "What's the big deal? Nobody had to know that."

"Except for the fact that Steve felt compelled to introduce himself that way. Let the harassment and chiding begin. And the girls at that school were unmerciful. They made me feel so bad. Like I couldn't get a date." Dana began to tear up, again.

"We left early and went to the House of Pancakes for dessert. Steve dropped me off and went home. I walked around the corner to Howard's house. I knew he'd be home. A school dance was not likely to be on his schedule. He had finally told me he was gay." Dana seemed to be self-satisfied with this, though she abruptly changed the subject back to her husband.

"I have to admit," Dana continued. "Andy has come a long way. "He could never consider it for himself, but he has finally come around to the idea that people don't necessarily choose their sexual preferences." Dana half smiled. "I remember when I asked him what he would do if one of our kids were to come out to us."

"What did he say?" Carmen showed great interest. She had been working with Andy on an individual basis, and after the money thing, she suggested he work with a male therapist to address some of his male ego issues. She wondered if he had become a little less stoic and conservative in his thinking.

"He said that he loves our kids, all three of them, no matter what." Dana was a little surprised when he said this, but was realizing that, about a lot of things, he wasn't such an ogre after all. "I'd have to get used to the idea, but it wouldn't change how I feel about them."

"I can speak for myself." Andy chimed in. "You two act like I'm not even in the room." Andy had agreed to come back to couples therapy after several sessions with his own doctor. Dana made him go. He didn't think he was the problem. Surprise! Dana was more sarcastic than ever when he said that. *They never do*, she thought.

"Sorry about that." Carmen laughed.

"Sorry, bud."

Carmen was going to let Dana lead, because it was she that wanted to unfold a few things, and had asked to have a buffer or safeguard if Andy got too angry or upset.

"So," Dana began. "I wanted to first tell you that I love you."

"Really, because you could have fooled me," barked Andy. "Come on, no nasty remarks. This is supposed to be a healing session. Let me at least get some of this out before you let loose at me." Dana took a deep breath. "There is a lot here, so please, Andy, be patient."

Carmen was gently nodding her head. She was glad to see Dana standing up for herself and handling the situation with aplomb. Her role as mediator has been getting easier and easier as Dana has been unfolding into this new version of herself. She made a mental note to mention that to Dana at some point.

Dana started over. "First, please know that I love you, but that you and I seem to express it in different ways." Carmen nodded her head. "For you, it seems like the amount of sex you get is directly related to how much I love you." There was silence. She went on. "For me, the actual sex is relatively unimportant. I feel like we are intimate in so many other ways."

"Wait, wait." Andy interrupted. "Isn't it the same thing? Sex and intimacy?"

"No, you can be intimate without ever even taking off your clothes." Carmen jumped in. "Intimacy, by definition, is a state marked by emotional closeness or warmth. Intercourse doesn't have to be involved." Oh well, she thought, that didn't take long.

"Damn." Andy was trying to be a little lighter now, and it was appreciated, however hesitantly.

Dana continued. "I show my love for you by cooking your favorite foods, by taking care of you when you're sick, by keeping your home. I even will buy you a Bulldog shirt or hat even though it pains me to do so." Dana watched for Andy's reaction. "I even sit there while you watch those silly TV shows, just to be in the same room with you." He rolled his eyes. "I think that says love."

Carmen stepped in. "Andy, Dana has a few things going on, that if you really understood, perhaps you wouldn't feel quite as distanced."

Andy sat up, worried. "Are you okay? Is something wrong?"

"Relax. You just need to be aware of a few things." Carmen continued. "Dana is a little uncomfortable with having intercourse these days. It's actually a physical thing that women go through at her stage in life. There are ways to get around it, but it's actually physically painful for her."

"I didn't know. I don't want to hurt her." He turned toward Dana. "You know I don't want to hurt you.

In her heart of hearts, Dana knew that. In fact, she sometimes wishes he would lighten up a little. She didn't need a knight in shining armor to protect her from everyone and everything. She was a big girl and could fight her own battles. At least she could, now, that she was sober, and a little surer of herself.

Carmen continued. "There is also the issue of her hesitancy since she got sober. She had some innate fears about having relations with being under the influence, and when Dana was drinking, she had considerably less inhibitions." Carmen looked over to Dana as if to get her approval. Dana nodded. "She also wanted you to know that sex was a way of keeping you at a distance from her drinking, so she wanted to keep you happy in the bedroom."

"Boy did she ever." Andy reflected back to the days when he was getting laid two and three times a day. It was a conundrum for him. He loved the sex, but he suspected it wasn't normal for Dana to be like that. He figured it was just a stage. He had liked to believe that women hit their sexual peak in their forties, because he read it somewhere ... He had no idea she was drinking as much as she was, so he was just going along for the ride.

He would be stretched out on the couch in the den watching television, relaxed after playing some morning tennis, taking a shower and having a light breakfast. It was the perfect time for a nap because the kids were all out somewhere, and except for the dog, they were alone in the house. Dana would inevitably come in from the back patio, where she had been "gardening." Suddenly she would be at the door, naked and sweaty. She would climb on top of him, ride him for a few minutes, and then leave him to take his nap. As fast as she had appeared, she was gone, and he would sleep really well.

He had no idea that there was a motive behind all of that. If he was asleep, she could actually drink from a glass instead of having to take swigs directly from the bottle. He had no idea that she would be drinking at eleven in the morning anyway.

By the time she was finished with the dinner dishes, Dana would have likely put down a pint and a half of whiskey, would have dispensed with the kids one way or another. She would have headed back to the bedroom with some seductive excuse, and of course, Andy would follow, locking the door. Their antics, their positions, and everything about what they were doing had been a blast, for Andy. Of course, Dana would wake up the next morning with no recollection of it, finding her clothes in a trail to the bed, and worrying what else she had done during that particular blackout.

"Dana is having some trouble relaxing about the sexual intimacy part, and because you are placing so much emphasis on it, she is pulling further and further away." Carmen was only repeating Dana's words. "You are right when you feel that. It is there. But it has nothing to do with whether or not she loves you."

"I don't even know where to start." Dana was pacing back and forth.

"Take your time." Andy was at the point where he would do anything to fix his marriage. His wife had quit drinking. He knew how hard that was. She had been working really hard with this therapist, so he knew she was serious too. "I promise I'm not going anywhere." Dana thought she saw tears welling up in his eyes. She knew better than to call attention to it. It would either embarrass him or evoke some lame joke about not telling anyone.

"There's just so much stuff in my past that shaped how I feel about men, about sex about myself … I'm not sure any man would have the patience to wait as I worked through it all." Dana fidgeted nervously.

"Dana, I don't want to sound corny, but I married you because I love you, for better or for worse. Whatever it is, we'll fix it together." Andy wasn't sure what he was in for, but he wanted to be a calming force. He wanted to be the knight in shining armor. That was his job.

Dana began to unfold to her husband as she had to her therapist all of the things by which she had been haunted. Her realization, finally, in middle age, is *that everyone has a past.* That's what makes them who they are. Everything that she has experienced is nothing really out the realm of ordinary. Most women have a laundry list much like hers. It was only now, as she was approaching middle age, going through the process of redefining herself, and with her newfound sobriety, that she had been able to accept and embrace it as part of who she was and is. She paused during her diatribe, with a sense of sorrow for the multitude of women who never figure this out. She had been so afraid to tell Andy about her experience with homosexuality because he had always been so judgmental about it. She now understood that while a lot of people experiment with things like that, some people take it further, and some people are, indeed, bi-sexual or homosexual. It doesn't have to be a stigma or a disgrace.

Andy had already made it abundantly clear that the things that happened to her between her and her father happened forty years ago and that he felt she should get over it. She was a little hesitant over this one, because this was not really a lesson Andy had figured out for himself yet, especially where financial insecurity was concerned. And who cares about the dating of other guys? She had him.

The one big deal she never had told him was about the molestation and the abuse. These were things that she had buried so deeply in the abyss of her psyche that she hadn't ever dealt with them before Carmen helped her put them in their proper place. She knew she could never give Andy specific details because she didn't want him to judge people or be vindictive. She had already seen how he can be malicious if someone hurts her or one of the kids.

"I can imagine how that could really shape your feelings about men." Andy was really shocked. "You could have just told me. It's me, remember?"

"First of all," began Dana, "I can never tell you who it was that messed with me when I was a kid. I don't want you to know that because I don't want it to change your feelings and demeanor with this person. And the date rape ... I got away from the guy, but it sure did color the way I felt about dating and sex."

Dana waited for a reaction, but Andy sat quietly, just listening. After all of the fighting over stupid things, it seemed like he really understood that sometimes he just needs to let her vent. Dana couldn't get over how attentive he was being.

"You know, my Dad could have made a big difference in how things turned out, that is, if he had been able to." Dana now approached the subject that she felt affected her the most. Her father. "I finally realized that he just couldn't. That serenity prayer that they say in Alcoholics Anonymous comes in handy."

"How do you mean?" asked Andy.

"I finally understand that Daddy did the best he could. We all do the best we can with what we've got." Dana always hated throwing the AA parlance at him, but in this case, it seemed fitting. "I finally let go of that, and instead of blaming him, I now am working on myself just to fix the things I feel are holding me back."

Again, Dana sat back and waited for a response. Andy was wordless. His eyes were slightly red, and she noticed a tear sneaking down the far side of his face. He tried so hard to never let her see him cry. "So now you know. Everything. I was so afraid it would change how you felt about me."

"Honey, nothing could do that. I love you." Andy was sincere. He didn't understand everything, but he was trying.

"Why, Andy? Why do you love me?" Dana really never knew the answer to this question. She was only beginning to learn to love herself.

"Uh-oh," he smiled. "I didn't know there was going to be a test." Dana smiled … or rather smirked. After twenty five years of living with this man, she had come to expect these kinds of answers, yet she loved them, and him. Andy Gordon had taught her, along with some of the other trials and tests she had faced, that life was always going to present challenges, but that you needed to face these challenges with a good sense of humor and the knowledge that together they would survive them. She had also learned never to do anything to sacrifice the integrity of her potential. Drinking, she found, would sacrifice all of it.

Dana and Andy left the session with Carmen together for the first time since their initial visit, and went home in one car.

"C'mon." Dana took Andy by the hand and led him back to the bedroom. "Let's take a nap." They climbed on top of the bed together, and spooning, fell off to sleep. Andy whispered in Dana's ear. "I love you Dana, I always will …"

Andy woke up an hour later, but Dana did not.

PART 3

CHAPTER 12

"**Y**ou wanna get locked up?" The cop yanked his arm away from Andy's grip. "Don't ever grab a police officer like that again."

"Sorry sir, but my wife hasn't come out of the building." Andy was now overcome with terror. He could hardly get the words out. "She … she … was following me down. We were up … Top of the … she was …" He was trying to hold back tears. "She was going to use the ladies room and then meet me down here. PLEASE. Somebody has to go in and find her."

The police officer turned and faced Andy, putting both hands on his shoulders. "Settle down. We have a team in there now. There's nobody in the restaurant. I'll have them check the restrooms." The officer slid the radio out of his belt with his right hand, keeping his left hand on Andy's shoulder. He was too experienced with this, having been a San Francisco Policeman for over twenty years. He had seen the best and the worst outcomes of these tremors. And this wasn't even a full-fledged earthquake … yet.

"Ground to 127. Are the restrooms clear upstairs? We have a report of a missing person." The officer turned to Andy.

"Description?" All of a sudden, Andy couldn't picture what his wife had been wearing. "She's my height, long, light brown hair … she's wearing it pulled back with one of those yarn things."

"What is she wearing?"

"Um … Uh … oh, she has a black … no grey dress on. And sandals." Andy had started pacing back and forth. Most of the people who he had seen in the restaurant had gone. The remainder of people milling around must have been hotel guests, all waiting patiently for that "all clear" to return to their rooms. He hadn't felt any further rumblings, and the sounds of the sirens had died down. Even the waitress had taken a seat on the sidewalk, up against the light post, and was calmly smoking a cigarette.

"No one in the restrooms," came the crackle from the police radio.

"Where could she be?" Andy was now choking on his words. He took off around to the back of the building. The doorman said there was a service entrance there. When he got to the side, they had put up barricades and would not let anyone through.

"Is there anyone back there who came out of the building?" Andy was screaming now. He never lost his composure so this kind of outburst was new to him. "PLEASE, I can't find my wife."

At the moment he said it, there was a pop and grind from the generator next to the building where the barricades stood. "Well, now that's a good sign," said yet another policeman. "No damage to the power grid in the area, or in the hotel."

Andy spun around and ran back to the front of the hotel. Out of breath, he found the doorman again. "Are they letting people back in?" he gasped.

"Not quite yet, sir." The doorman was doing his best to hold the crowd back. "Please hold on ladies and gentlemen, until the police and fire personnel come out and give us the all clear."

The waiting was agonizing. "Want a smoke?" Andy and Dana's waitress had come up behind him and offered him the only thing she could. "It always calms me down."

"I don't smoke, but thanks."

"She's okay. They'll find her."

"Thanks." Andy was trying as hard as he could to believe that.

What had seemed like a lifetime had only been twenty minutes when a fireman in full gear came out of the front of the building holding his hat. He leaned over and put the hat between his legs, and began motioning to the truck parked in front, waving his arms in a crossing pattern over his head, and then motioning with his hands towards the hotel.

"What's that mean? What's he doing? What's that mean?" Andy grabbed the doorman by the arm.

"That usually means someone is stuck in the elevator, but that the rest of the building is safe. We still have to wait outside."

"It's Dana, I know it. Aww, and she hates elevators. She's probably having a wicked panic attack." Andy followed the two firemen that were running from the truck. "Can I go with you? I think that's my wife in there."

"Wait here and we'll call you if we need you." The firemen glanced at each other, knowing full well that this guy would be nothing but an impediment to their work. Telling him they might need him might make him back off.

"It's caught between three and four. Looks like the cable slipped." The fireman pressed his ear against the door on the third floor. "I don't hear anything, but that doesn't mean there isn't someone in there. Call in rescue just to be on the safe side." The fireman pulled a tire iron out of his pack, and tried to wedge the door open.

"Careful." The hotel manager screamed as he came running out of the stairwell. "Don't bust it up. It's an antique."

"Huh? Really? I should protect your antique when there might be someone's life on the line?" He elbowed the policeman behind him. "Get this guy outta here."

The door opened slowly, two or three inches, and in the darkness, the fireman was able to make out the image of Dana's purse, pressed up against the back wall. "There's definitely someone or something there. Hand me the flashlight." The floor of the elevator sat about chest high. When the light hit the wall, the fireman saw not only the purse, but Dana's lifeless arm lying next to it.

"Quick, get me that short ladder." He pried the door open wide enough to wedge his arms in. "Put it here where I can get up and get some leverage." He climbed up two steps and using his elbows, he wedged the door open further. "Where's emergency already?"

The siren was blasting as it pulled in the driveway and around the circle, nearly taking out some of the remaining hotel guests. Most had walked to nearby restaurants that were already up and running, if for no other reason than to have a place to sit down while they waited. The emergency personnel jumped out, opened the back of the vehicle, and grabbed a gurney and some other equipment. As they hurried toward the front door, Andy accosted them.

"Who's in there? Who's hurt?" He tried to keep up with them, but once again, the doorman stopped him.

"Andy!" The doorman had spent enough time with Andy to know his name, that he and Dana lived in Atlanta and that they were on their honeymoon. "Son, let them do their jobs."

By the time the emergency crew arrived on the third floor, one of the firemen had been able to climb up inside the elevator and was at Dana's side. "She's got a pulse, however weak. She's breathing lightly. There's a little blood, I think from her ear. Don't know if it's a cut or from inside."

"Don't touch her. Don't move her." Nick, the skinnier of the two EMT's hopped up into the elevator and reached back for his bag. He quickly took her vitals. "Hand me a neck brace. I don't think there are any broken bones here, but it looks like she hit her head pretty bad." He carefully slipped the brace under her hair and gently fastened it. She was breathing, but didn't react to anything he did. "Slide the board in. Why no emergency light in here?"

Between the two firefighters and the two EMT's, it took a total of three minutes to gingerly roll Dana onto the board, slide it through the wedged elevator doors, and gently place it on the gurney. They were in and out of the building in less than five minutes. Carrying the gurney with Dana strapped to it, they dropped the wheels when they got to the bottom of the stairs.

Andy met them there, breathless. "Is she okay? Is she breathing?" He was inconsolable. "Is she dead?" He grabbed hold of the gurney as they hurriedly rolled it toward the ambulance. "Can I go with you? I don't have a car. I have to go with you."

One of the policemen dropped back. "Sir, let them get her situated. You can ride to the hospital with them but let them get her in first."

"Can somebody at least tell me if she's going to be okay?" "We're doing what we can." The EMT answered in a matter-of-fact way. Doing this every day for a living made him indifferent to the people around him. He knew he had a job to do, and wasn't tuned in to the emotions of victims or anyone else involved. "Do me a favor. Let us work and ask the doctor when we get to the emergency room." Andy climbed in the back and sat on a narrow bench in the corner. He reached for Dana's lifeless hand and held it as the medic put an oxygen mask over her mouth and nose. He hadn't seen her that pale since the time she was at the top of the escalator of the football stadium and lost her balance, thinking she was falling. It was that same ashen, pasty look that she always gets when she's having anxiety. But this time, her lips were bright red, not grey. How strange, he thought, to be wearing lipstick now. Dana hates lipstick.

One of the policemen tossed Dana's purse on the floor of the vehicle before he slammed the doors shut. Before Andy could bend over to pick it up, the ambulance lurched forward and was on its way, sirens shrieking. That was the only sound Andy could hear, besides his own heart hammering a beat in his chest, saying "Hang on, hang on, hang on …"

The next time Andy saw Dana after they propelled her away at the Emergency Room entrance, was through a double thick glass retaining wall, separating him, unmercifully, from the love of his life, and sending him reeling into all kinds of nightmarish thoughts. This was Dana's way of dealing with things, not mine, he thought. He shook his head violently. "Hold on to yourself. Someone has to be the voice of reason, here." He spoke aloud, as if someone was there. It was only Andy, with his arms pressed against the glass, crossed over his head, his hands placed gently on the back of his head. He had reverted to something he used to do as a child. He was twirling his curly hair with his index fingers, as he did when he was a toddler, to help himself calm down and go to sleep.

There would be little sleep tonight, he thought. It was already ten, California time. He hadn't even thought to call Atlanta to let everyone know what's going on. He could just picture his mother-in-law, waiting by the phone in the kitchen. I'm sure she was watching the news all night. They had reported that it was a mild tremor, so she can't possibly be too worried, he thought. If she gets worse, he'll call. If she gets better, no need to upset them.

"Can I get you a cup of coffee, at least?" The nurse who was at the central desk in the Intensive Care Unit hadn't been very nice to him before. She hadn't let him near Dana when they were bringing her up from the emergency room. Why was she being so nice now?

"Is the cafeteria open this late?"

"No," she said. "It closed at nine, but we have a fresh pot brewing in the ICU waiting room. I just thought since you won't go wait in there, I'd bring you some."

"Thanks. That would be nice." Andy hadn't eaten anything but two crab claws and a glass and a half of champagne since that burger at the winery. He wasn't very hungry, though. "Nothing in it, thanks." Dana was completely still, with all kinds of tubes and wires coming out of her. The monitors were beeping and clicking, and the oxygen pump was slow and steady in its laboring to breathe for her. She wasn't this bad when they brought her in, Andy thought. Did something happen behind the ER's closed doors? There was an awful lot of running in and out and back and forth. Andy had never been this close to a trauma before.

"Here you go, Mr. Gordon." The nurse handed the coffee to Andy. "Why don't you try to relax a little? You can watch some television or read a magazine to take your mind off of things."

"Maybe not such a bad idea after all." Andy followed the nurse back to the waiting room. There was one other man in there, sound asleep, snoring steadily with his head tilted against the wall and a newspaper bunched up on his lap. The mint green walls cast a strange pallor on his face, reminding Andy of the lighting in the wine cellar they had visited. When was that? Was it yesterday? Two days ago? No, that was just today. Andy felt like he had been riding on that mountain highway without a seatbelt. Maybe his skin was green, too.

As he fell into a chair, he heard a flurry of activity just outside the waiting room door. One of the monitors in one of the rooms had changed from a steady beat to a very high pitched screech. Andy knew it couldn't be Dana. He had just left her. She was fine. It was Dana. No it wasn't. Couldn't be. She's fine. She's going to be great. We have a whole life ahead of us. What if she's not?

The back and forth in his head was driving his feet faster and faster back to the window. There were at least six white coats surrounding her bed. Suddenly, someone jumped on top of her, while someone else got on the phone, while still someone else rolled a silver cart over to the bedside.

"Code Blue, ICU-two, Code Blue, ICU two." Andy couldn't believe it. It was as if he was watching an episode of Medical Center. But there was no Chad Everett. And there were no commercials. Why did Dana like those doctor shows anyway? All they did for him was give him way too much information to think about now.

Just as the one doctor approached her with those paddle things, the other doctor jumped off. They're not all doctors, Andy thought. This isn't happening. He dropped the cup of coffee and began banging on the glass. "What's happening? What's going on? Is she okay?" The nurse who brought the coffee had her arm around him trying to turn him away from the glass. Another nurse drew the curtains so he could no longer see. Andy was frantic. "Please, God, oh please …"

Andy dropped to his knees, in the puddle of coffee, and began sobbing uncontrollably. "Please don't let her die. We haven't even had a chance to start. It can't be over."

Dana's body jumped with the touch of the paddles.

Get off of me Andy, she thought. Although she couldn't hear anything specific, she knew there was somebody in the room besides Andy and her. There's somebody else in the house. Andy, you need to go check it out. Dana was thinking that he would probably just get up, lock the bedroom door and call the police.

"She's got normal rhythm." The medical workers who had surrounded Dana's bed slowly peeled away. "Everything looks okay."

"That was weird," said one of the nurses. "It was like she was dreaming or something. What did the neurologist say about her brain activity?"

"Not in the chart yet," said another nurse.

The desk nurse helped Andy from the floor and got him some paper towels. "Come on, son," she whispered, "You look like you had an accident. You and I know it's coffee. Let's get you some scrubs to change into."

Andy slowly got up from the floor, first to his knees, and then, with a wobble, to his feet. He felt the blood rushing up the back of his head and a throbbing in his chest.

"She's okay." The nurse opened the curtains. Dana was peacefully sleeping, and all of the beeps and clicks were back to a steady pace.

Andy took the scrubs, and hesitantly ventured into the men's room. Whatever little was in his stomach, came violently up as he heaved and sobbed for a few minutes, partly out of relief, and partly still in shock. He glanced at himself in the mirror, noting that he was, indeed, green.

Andy finally dozed off on the couch in the waiting room after several more hours of standing against the window watching Dana sleep. Or was she sleeping. The doctors had not told him anything other than the fact that she had a serious head injury, and that there had been some bleeding on the brain. Even the thing with the paddles and the frickin silver cart hadn't been explained, other than she needed some help with steadying her heart beat. What the hell was that supposed to mean? Did she have a heart attack? And why is she on that breathing thing? And the bleeding in the brain … is there brain damage? Nobody tells you anything around here.

It was six thirty in the morning when Andy finally awoke. He had rolled over and fallen off of the couch. Grateful that there were a few cushions on the floor, he reached for his trousers that had been drying out over a chair, and went out into the central area to use the men's room. The curtains on the ICU were closed. His heart skipped a beat and he lunged toward the desk. "Is Dana okay?"

The charge nurse, a different one, said "Curtains are only closed because the physicians are doing rounds. Not to worry."

Andy continued on to the men's room but turned back. "If I go in there, will you be sure the doctor doesn't leave before I speak with him?"

"Yes sir, Mr. Gordon. I'll be sure you get a chance to talk to him." Andy used the facilities and had on his own clothes in record time. He was back in front of the nurse's station in less than two minutes. "Mr. Gordon?" Dr. Goldstein walked toward the desk. "I'm Aaron Goldstein. I've been keeping an eye on your wife." He offered his hand, but Andy had no interest in being cordial. He wanted answers.

A barrage of questions followed. "Is she going to be okay? What happened with her heart last night? Is her brain still bleeding? Why can't she breathe on her own? Can I go in and see her? Is she just sleeping or what? Can I be with her and hold her hand? Does she need me to donate blood?"

"Whoa, whoa, whoa. Slow down." Dr. Goldstein could barely keep track. Andy was coming at him from all directions.

"First, let me tell you that she took a pretty bad hit to her head. There was a small bleed, but that has subsided." Andy let out a big sigh.

"That doesn't mean she is in a safe zone ... yet."

Andy's sigh was short lived, and while he didn't panic just yet, he held his breath waiting for the next question to be answered.

"Dana has a small amount of swelling of the brain. It will take some time for that to dissipate before we really know if there are going to be any long term effects from the injury." The doctor continued. "What she has is kind of like a bad concussion. The problem is that she isn't waking up from it quick enough for my comfort. By all measure, she is in fact, in a coma."

"A coma! Geez... For how long?" Andy now had a whole new set of questions. "I mean, how long will it take for the swelling to go down? Is that why she's on the breathing machine?"

Dr. Goldstein put an arm around Andy's shoulder. "Let's go sit down." He nudged Andy towards an unoccupied corner of the reception area. As they sat, Dr. Goldstein continued. "She could wake up while we're sitting here, or she could be out of it for weeks. You never can tell. It all depends on her."

A nurse brought over a tray with two cups of coffee and two small pieces of Danish. Andy was ravenous. "Thank you." He nearly stuffed the entire pastry in his mouth at once. "And the heart?"

Dr. Goldstein took a small sip of coffee. "That was a fluke." Her heart is perfectly strong. In fact, we were planning on taking her off the oxygen and all monitors except the usual vitals, or we were, until that happened." He took another sip. "There was nothing to point to why that happened. Her heart skipped a few beats, seemed to have stopped for just a second or two, and then recovered." He was shaking his head as if he was baffled, himself. "It may have been an aberration; it may have just been a glitch in the equipment when she was first hooked up to it."

"Never seen this before," he continued. She has a normal, strong heartbeat and has since we got her up here from the ER. When they found her yesterday, it was steady, but a little weak, perhaps due to the trauma." He took one last gulp from the coffee cup. "I'm confident that her heart is fine. Now we play the waiting game. I'm going to leave her on monitors through the day. If there aren't any more episodes like last night, we'll discuss taking her off tomorrow."

"Tomorrow! Then you don't think she'll wake up today." Andy decided he better call her folks. And for that matter, his.

"Mom?" Andy's voice faltered. He didn't quite know what he was going to say, but he knew he couldn't go another minute dealing with this alone. He had never faced anything like this before. Even when the dog died, he had run away to do it. Nobody actually had to watch it happen. What was he thinking? Dana is NOT going to die. She's going to wake up and be fine.

"Andy. What's the matter? We didn't think we'd be hearing from you until you got home." Andy's mother was the exact opposite of Marge. She never showed emotion, and was not reactive to any situation. This was good for Andy, because she wasn't an alarmist, and certainly, she would be a calming factor for him. "You weren't near any of that tremor thing, were you?"

"Well, um, as a matter of fact, we were," And started. He took a large gulp of air. "Dana was in an elevator when it happened." He got the first part out safely.

"Is she okay?"

"Well, um," he continued. "Not really." Andy felt himself welling up. He didn't want to let on that he was falling apart. "She hit her head pretty badly. They said the elevator slipped on the cable and dropped a few floors." He paused. "She's in a coma, Mom."

"Oh, my." Sandra sat up straight. "Do you need us to come out there?"

"I haven't called Dana's parents yet. I'm sure they'll be coming." Andy didn't want to be overwhelmed, and he knew Marge and his mom didn't see eye to eye. The last thing he wanted was to feel that tension. "Let me call you later and see how things play out. The doctor said she could wake up today. They're doing some neurological studies this morning to see how her brain is doing."

"Okay, you just let us know what you want. We're here."

"Thanks, mom."

Andy put the receiver back in the pay phone slot. He reached into his pocket for some more change, but couldn't find anything but a few pennies. What a jerk, he thought. Why didn't I call Dana's parents first? Sometimes I don't think.

Andy tripped down the two flights of stairs to the cafeteria to get something to eat, some coffee, and more importantly, some change. He put the food on a corner table and went looking for a pay phone.

"Mrs. James? It's Andy."

Marge went instantly into panic mode. "What's the matter?" She immediately thought back to the time Dana had been rear-ended in that little sardine can of a car Ben had gotten for the kids. The girl that called her was fine, but why hadn't Dana called her. She had pictured her lying in the street.

"Are you okay? Is Dana okay? I knew something had happened when I saw the news. You were in the earthquake weren't you?" Marge's bombardment of questions reminded Andy of how he had been with the doctor last night.

"Dana was in the elevator at the Mark Hopkins hotel, coming down to meet me. She hit her head pretty badly. She's in a coma, Mrs. James"

"Why didn't you call sooner? I could have come out to be with you?" Marge was standing up reaching for the phone book. "I'm booking a flight as soon as possible. What hospital?"

"Geez, I don't even know. I rode with the ambulance and I've been here all night." Andy covered the mouthpiece and called over to someone standing in line in the cafeteria. "What hospital is this?"

"San Francisco General"

"Thanks." Andy returned to the call. "San Francisco General. It's right near the Mark, but don't stay there."

Marge could barely wait to hang up to make her travel arrangements. This was her baby, her only little girl. She knew Ben would find a reason not to go. He was never good with hospitals. She found the phone number for United and booked a flight that left in less than two hours. She was on her way.

When Andy returned to the table where he had left his breakfast, it was gone. "Crap!" He didn't know whether someone had lifted it or if they just thought it was left there and they cleaned it up. "Damn it." He decided it wasn't worth waiting in line, and he didn't want to miss Dr. Goldstein, so he returned to the stairwell and hopped up the stairs, two at a time, till he reached the third floor ICU unit.

"Where is she?" The curtains were open, but Dana was no longer in bed two.

The nurse called over to Andy, "They took her down for her brain scan. She should be gone about an hour." Andy dropped his shoulders and his head and scuffed his feet over to the waiting room, collapsing into the couch where he had spent the night.

Could you turn down the volume a little Matthew? Dana lay still in the chamber, but her mind was racing. *Matthew was blaring his stereosome kind of noise from a band called Linkin Park. It's not me, mom, it's the girls. Dana should have known. Matthew has excellent taste in music. He even likes old Sinatra tunes.*

The nurse slid Dana out of the tube on the table. She remained lifeless, but breathing on her own this morning, and her heart beating strong. "Doctor Ferrer? Did you notice her eyelids?"

Dr. Eugene Ferrer was a world renowned neurologist whom Dr. Goldstein had called in that morning to run these tests. He had only been and SF GEN for a few months, but they had become fast friends. "That confirms what I'm seeing here. She's got normal brain activity. She should be coming out of this. I want to find out what the holdup is. The swelling is subsided, so there is something else going on." He crossed his arms, with one hand resting on his chin. "I'll consult with Dr. Goldstein and perhaps run some more tests this afternoon. They can take her back upstairs."

When the orderly rolled Dana back into the ICU, Andy noticed immediately that they did not hook her up to as many machines. *That's a very good sign,* he thought. *Maybe she's getting better.* He left the glass for a minute and approached the nurse's station.

"Is there any chance at all I can go in to be with her?"

"Yes, actually. Let them get her settled in. You should know, though, that if there is any kind of emergency with any of the patients, or any kind of procedure that has to be done, you'll be asked to leave." The nurse methodically explained the rules. Nobody ever listened to her anyway. Whenever she had to ask someone to leave the bedside of a loved one, she almost always had a battle on her hands. She understood why, but it was very frustrating, none-the-less.

Andy waited patiently. He hadn't even been able to stroke her cheek since before they left for the Mark. He just wanted to let her know he was there.

After five minutes, the nurse called him in. "You can sit beside her, and you may hold her hand ... her left one. Talk to her softly. That might help." The nurse backed away, watching as Andy delicately lifted Dana's limp hand into his, and placed his other on top. Their two shiny gold wedding bands caught the dim light of the Intensive Care Unit, sparkling, giving Andy an imaginary sense of comfort.

Hours passed. Nurses and doctors, orderlies and maintenance men, were coming and going. Andy thought to himself that I guess everyone is doing okay because there haven't been any emergencies or procedures. Just as he said it, though, a buzzer went off two beds away. True to her word, the nurse asked Andy to leave. He did, begrudgingly, and parked himself in front of the glass, at least until they closed the curtains.

Andy was getting hungry. Thinking that was a good sign, he went downstairs to find a sandwich. He hadn't realized that it was already mid-afternoon. There wasn't much left from which to choose so he grabbed the first normal sandwich he could find. California is weird, he thought. There was a cooler of soda by the cash register. This time, he didn't put the food down. He paid for it and took it back upstairs with him.

Marge was waiting for him in the ICU waiting room. "Oh Andy! Are you okay? How is she doing?"Andy didn't have a second to process the fact that his mother-in-law was already there. He put the food down on the end table, and reached out to hug her.

"Less than 24 hours ago we were getting ready to go out for a drink and then on a tour of San Francisco by night." He started to weep. "It seems like an eternity since then. I think this is the first real food I've even considered eating since then."

Andy sat down on the edge of the couch and began to fill Marge in on all he knew. "She had the neurological studies this morning, but I haven't seen Dr. Goldstein since very early, so I don't know the results, prognosis, anything." He wondered if he should even mention the thing about her heart. Marge didn't need to know this; it was one more thing for her to wield her hysteria. He decided not to, since she's been fine since, and she's not on those machines anymore. The cardiologist looked at her late last night and gave her a good report.

"As of last night, there was still some swelling around the brain. She had had a tiny bit of bleeding, but that apparently stopped. We're waiting for the swelling to go down. The neurologist should be able to tell us if there's any damage."

Marge gasped. "Brain damage? Oh no, oh my God, no." Her face was panic-stricken, and frozen that way. All Marge could think of was how bright and talented her daughter is, and how this whole thing is absolutely devastating.

"Wait, Mrs. James. They don't know that yet. She might be just fine." Andy was immediately sorry he said this. Marge is just like Dana when it came to things like this. She always jumps to conclusions and fears the worst. "All I said is that they were TESTING to see. I have faith that she's going to be fine. Remember its Dana. She's way too hard headed to let a little bump on the head bring her down."

Marge looked at Andy, her face falling from panic, and rising into a smile. "Thank you Andy. Just … thank you."

The charge nurse opened the curtain to the glass and then poked her head in the waiting room. Mr. Gordon, you may go back in now, if you'd like."

"This is Dana's mom. Can she come too?"

"You can visit one at a time. Mrs. uh …" "James," offered Marge.

"Mrs. James, the rules are as follows. You must be very quiet. If there is an emergency with another patient or a procedure needs to be done, you will be asked to leave." The nurse was beginning to sound like a robot.

"I'm just grateful to be able to get in to see her," said Marge. "Please. Show me the way."

Andy watched through the glass as Marge leaned over her daughter and kissed her on the forehead. Did he see the sheet move at the foot of the bed? No, that was because Marge was leaning on it. It was nothing. She is still asleep.

I love you too, mom, thought Dana. I'm so glad you get along so well with Andy. Dana was forever going to remember this moment. He asked me to marry him. She thought. Marge started to cry. I'm so happy for you, my baby girl.

Marge started to cry. "Please wake up, my baby girl. Please." Marge teetered backwards and shrank down into the chair. She held Dana's hand in hers and wept silently.

Don't cry mom, Dana thought. This is a happy time. You finally get to plan a wedding. Don't cry.

Andy couldn't bear watching much longer. He left the window and went back into the waiting room, and picked up a copy of TV Guide. At least he could watch M.A.S.H. while he was waiting there tonight. He didn't want to take any time away from Marge, but he wanted to get in there and be with his wife.

After tapping on Andy's shoulder for a few seconds, Marge realized that he must be totally exhausted and decided to let him sleep. She backed away and quietly left him in the waiting room, tip-toeing toward the nurse's station.

"I'm going to go find a hotel for the night. I don't think he's going to want to leave her, but just in case, can I have the phone number and extension to your desk so I can let him know where I am." She rifled through her purse looking for a pen and something on which to write. "I don't want to wake him. He's sleeping so soundly, and it doesn't look like there's going to be much of a change between now and the morning."

Marge jotted down the information the nurse was giving her when suddenly a buzzer went off in the ICU. "Excuse me," said the nurse. "I'll be right back." She jumped up from her chair and scooted around the counter, stopping first to close the curtains, and then around the side to the door of the unit. Marge was paralyzed by the noise and activity.

Andy heard it too, and flew out of the waiting room. "Is it Dana? Is she okay? What's going on?" Andy saw Marge at the desk, and assuming she was asked to leave the room, he panicked. "Was her buzzer going off?"

"I … I don't know." Marge stuttered. This was the first time she had to deal with this. "I was going to let you sleep and go find a hotel." She rested her arm across her purse, which was now splayed across the top of the counter. "I assumed you would want to stay with her ... I didn't think ..."

Andy was still somewhat groggy. He tried to process what Marge was saying. He was tired, hungry, and worried, and he felt dirty, as if he hadn't showered in days. "Where are you staying?"

"I don't know yet. I'm going to see if I can find a motel nearby.

Do you want a room? Or do you want to stay here?"

"Can you get a suite kind of room with couch or something? Or a cheaper motel? I can't afford any of these fancy places, but I really need a shower."

"Oh, Andy, don't be silly. I'll take care of it." Just as Marge finished her sentence, the door of the ICU flew open.

"Mr. Gordon, come quick," shouted the nurse. She held the metal door wide open as Andy scrambled through.

"What ... what ...?" cried Andy. As he turned the corner, he saw the end of Dana's bed and was able to detect movement of the sheets. "She's awake?"

"No, but we think she's almost there." The nurse could barely contain her joy. "She was mumbling something in her sleep. Her heart rate is faster, she seems to be taking deeper breaths. By the way, do you know someone named Carmen?"

Marge had her hands pressed against the window of the Intensive Care Unit, having ripped apart the curtains. Her eyes were filled with tears.

"Thank you so much. You know my mother, Andy and I all feel that you pretty much saved my life."

"No, Dana, you saved your own life. I'm just grateful to have met you. I've learned so much from you." Carmen didn't usually get so entrenched with a family like she had with the Gordons. She had, from the beginning, told Dana that she was old enough and had been in practice enough that she could break the rules. "You've worked very hard to get to this point. You've made great strides. You have come so far and are so well. That doesn't mean you won't have issues. We all have issues, but it's truly amazing how far you have come."

Dana crossed her legs under the sheets. Andy actually jumped back. "Did you see that?" He got in close to Dana's face. "Honey it's me, Andy. Wake up, Dana, it's me."

"You say that as if I'm fine. I'm not fine," said Dana, smugly. She turned toward her car. "But at least now I know how to muddle through stuff without hurting myself or anyone else."

"There will always be things that come up in life. I think the one thing you've learned is that all of the experiences you've had are what made you who you are. You've learned from them, they've made you strong." Carmen knew this was her swan song, her chance to drive the point home. "You have a lot of people you can call on but you can only rely on yourself. Nobody can define who you are but you. You are worthy, capable, and very special. Remember that."

"I will. I love you, Carmen. Thank you. I think it's time for me to go back, now."

"I love you too, Dana. Say hi to Andy for me."

"Dana, are you there? Who is Carmen?" Dana was completely still again. She was not moving, and her breathing had steadied. Andy started to back away, his optimism waning. "She's not going to wake up, is she?" he asked the nurse.

"Just the fact that there was movement before is good. She might just be dreaming. That means her brain is working." The nurse was trying not to show her disappointment. She really thought that if the husband came in and the patient heard his voice, she would wake up. She had seen it before several times.

"Let me go out and tell my mother-in-law what's going on." Andy was going to be as optimistic and show as much courage as he could muster. He pushed on the heavy metal door and started out, but was met by an anxious Marge.

"Was there something wrong? The nursed jumped when she heard the buzzer."

"Nothing wrong, in fact, something good." What he was going to tell her, he didn't yet know. "Come on, let's sit down." He took Marge by the elbow and led her to the same corner of the reception area where he had sat the night before with Dr. Goldstein.

"She seems to be starting to wake up. While I couldn't get her to open her eyes, the nurse said she was talking in her sleep, and starting to move around in the bed." Andy was trying to sound confident. "That's supposed to be a really good sign."

The tension, which only a moment ago was palpable, was leaving Marge's face. She was beginning to show the same signs of exhaustion as Andy. She dropped her shoulders and sank back into the chair. Her tears were coming steadily, although they were, this time, a reflection of relief, not fear.

"She's obviously getting better, Mom. I knew she would." Andy was starting to believe his own words. "Why don't we get that hotel thing settled and then go have some dinner?"

"There's an apartment hotel about a quarter of a mile up the street," offered the nurse. I have their phone number, if you'd like." It wasn't unusual for patient families to want to stay near when they had a loved one in the ICU, so the nurses had a list of resources at the station for all kinds of things. "They don't have a regular restaurant on site, but there are a few between here and there, and they do have a luncheonette that's open from six a.m. till about three." She was almost as disappointed as Andy and Marge. Doris had seen enough heartache working in the ICU. She loved happy endings. "Here, let me dial for you."

Andy took the phone from her. "Thank you so much." He put both his elbows on the counter and rested his head against the receiver.

"Good evening, I wondered if you had any rooms available for tonight." Andy paused and said, "I'll take it. We should be there to check in by seven. The name is Gordon." Andy handed the receiver back to the nurse, turned to Marge, who had remained glued to her chair, and said, "Done!"

After a light dinner they picked up at a deli on the walk to the hotel, both Andy and Marge collapsed into a state of numbness. They turned on the television, spoke not a word and agonized within their own minds for hours.

"Marge?" Andy said softly. "She's going to be okay, right?"

"Oh Andy, of course she is." It was Marge's turn to be the strong one. They seem to have been holding each other up throughout the afternoon and evening. "Why don't you go take a warm shower and try to get some sleep. I'm sure if there is any change, they'll call us from the hospital."

"That sounds really good to me." Andy slowly got up and wandered toward the bathroom. The room was not bad. He planned on sleeping on the couch in the sitting room, and Marge would use the bedroom. It was small, but she would have more privacy. Besides, he would be closer to the phone. The shower, however, was in her bathroom. "I'll make it quick."

Marge kicked off her pumps and curled her legs up under her on the couch. She didn't mean to, but she began to doze off while waiting for Andy. Her mind drifted back to when Dana was a little girl, how she would climb up on the piano bench next to Ben, and they would sing together or how she would torment her brothers and get them in trouble, thinking she was getting away with it. I knew who was doing what to whom, Marge thought. She was a little conniver, my baby. That's why she's been so successful in business so far. A smile came across Marge's face as she fell off to sleep.

Andy's mind was in a different place altogether. If only I had stayed upstairs with her, he thought. This never would have happened. I had to go on ahead, like I was on a mission or something. Andy didn't usually think that deeply about things, but this was his wife. This was the love of his life, lying in a hospital, and while she was doing better tonight, and he did feel somewhat hopeful, he just couldn't stand to see her this way. He had promised love her to take care of her for the rest of their lives only a few days ago.

Andy turned around in the shower and got a face full of soapy water as the shampoo ran down his face. He had thought he heard the phone ring. He opened the shower door and called out to Marge. "Was that the hospital?"

Marge was still asleep. Andy was hearing things. Maybe it was the water in his ears. He finished up in the shower, dried off and put back on the same clothes. "Oh, Crap." All of our stuff is over at the Jack Tar. I never called there."

"Hello. My name is Gordon. I'm in room 613. We've had an accident, and my wife is over at San Francisco General. I need to have our belongings sent over to me at the Mission Inn over by the Hospital and check out from there. Any way that can happen? You have my credit card."

"And your last name, Gordon?" came a voice on the other end of the line.

Andy was agitated. "That is my last name. Mr. and Mrs. Andrew Gordon. Room 613. May I speak with your manager please?" Andy was one of those people that had to go right to the top to get things done. He was imagining Dana getting frustrated with him because he was being short with the young lady who answered the phone.

The luggage arrived within the hour, and the driver had a receipt for Andy to sign, checking the Gordons out of room 613 of the Jack Tar Hotel after only 1 night. Here it was the third night of his honeymoon and he was sharing a room with his mother-in-law.

Marge had slept through the whole process. Andy went back into the bathroom, put on a pair of pajamas, and checked on Marge once more. Still asleep, he hadn't the heart to wake her. He shifted her legs to the side, allowing her to stretch out on the couch, carefully removed her glasses and put them on the side table. Andy found a light weight blanket at the end of the bed, and gently unfolded over Marge. Like Dana, she was a deep sleeper. Andy climbed into the bed in the other room and curled up around the pillow. It was almost midnight, and he was going to have to face another night without Dana.

CHAPTER 13

As if it were just another day of vacation, Andy was up at the crack of dawn, showered and dressed and ready to leave for the hospital. It was five thirty in the morning, and Marge hadn't moved. He had heard her late the night before, talking to Ben on the phone. Mr. James wasn't coming out to California unless Dana took a turn for the worse, he gathered, so he and Marge would have to hold each other up. Andy never understood how Ben was not too available to his family, but Dana had told him, once, that her Dad had a thing about hospitals. His beloved Dana and his future children would never know that feeling. He was going to make sure of it.

He waited quietly in the bedroom for a short time, but after a while, he couldn't contain himself, and went out to wake Marge. He wanted to get over to the hospital as soon as possible. It was a good sign that nobody had called from the hospital. Or was it?

"Mrs. James … Mrs. James … It's time to get up." Andy gently jostled Marge on the shoulder. The blanket he had used to cover her was in a heap on the floor. She was still fully dressed in yesterday's clothes.

"What time is it?" Marge was not a morning person. She hadn't even opened her eyes, but Andy recognized her horror when he told her it was only a few minutes after six. "Let me get my bearings."

"Tell you what. I'll go find some coffee while you shower and dress. We can be at the hospital by seven or so. Dr. Goldstein will be making rounds by half after." Andy was out the door before Marge could respond.

The city was still asleep as they walked the quarter mile to the hospital. It was a cool September morning. Marge was glad she had brought a jacket with her, and Andy was still pulling confetti out of the pockets of his as they walked up the inclined driveway to the front entrance to the hospital. "Sorry about that," Marge apologized. "It doesn't even seem funny right now."

"It's okay. We got a good laugh out of it." He added, "Three times."

They caught an elevator almost immediately, and Dr. Goldstein happened to be riding with them.

"Good morning Mr. Gordon." Dr. Goldstein was alone this time.

No students, no interns and no Specialists.

"Call me Andy. Dr. Goldstein, I'd like you to meet Dana's mother, Mrs. James." Andy was trying to hold back the questions with small talk, but he could almost feel them erupting. "Did you see her last night? Have you been up there yet this morning? She seemed to be better to me before we left last night? Did the nurse tell you what happened? Did you get the results of the neuro studies?"

"Andy, Andy, I haven't had my first cup of coffee yet." Dr. Goldstein was smiling. "Nice to meet you Mrs. James, although I would have preferred it to be under different circumstances."

"What does that mean?" asked Andy. "Has something changed?"

"No, Andy," Marge responded. "The doctor was just being polite.

Calm down." It was Marge's turn to be the voice of reason. "It's hard to believe you've only had one cup of coffee this morning!"

The elevator doors opened on the third floor and the three of them walked out together right into the reception area of the Intensive Care Unit. Dr. Goldstein went straight to the desk, spoke a moment with the nurse, who had just come on shift, and then entered the unit. The curtains were closed, so Andy and Marge took seats in the waiting room.

After ten minutes, which to Andy and Marge seemed like hours, Dr. Goldstein emerged from the unit and joined them in the waiting room. "I could probably go over all of the tests and give you my assessment, but there's time for that. Why don't you go in and have a visit now, while it's still quiet up here, and we can talk in a few minutes."

Andy jumped up and all but ran to the heavy metal door. Marge followed, clutching her purse against her chest. Dr. Goldstein lagged behind.

"Dana? It's me, your Honey bear," Andy stood beside the bed, watching his wife intently.

"Sweetie, Mommy's here too." Marge wasn't sure she was allowed in at the same time, so she stood back at the foot of the bed."

"And where's Dad?" Dana mumbled, still with her eyes closed.

"What? Did you say that? Did you say 'where's dad'?" Andy wasn't sure he actually heard it.

"Mm Hmm." Dana's monitor blipped up to a slightly higher level for three or four seconds, and then returned back to a slow, steady pace.

Dr. Goldstein stepped closer. "I wanted her to be the one to tell you. But she needs to go back to sleep." Apparently, she woke up about two hours ago. I got a call from the night nurse that she was having some kind of nightmare, and she was talking in her sleep. It woke her." Dr. Goldstein was grinning from ear to ear. "We need to let her rest for a while until she wakes up on her own again. Let's go out and talk."

Andy and Marge were both in tears and reaching for each other to hug. They barely heard a word the doctor said. He repeated himself. "We need to let her rest for a while until she wakes up on her own again. Let's the three of us go back out into the waiting room and talk."

"We're going to run the same battery or neurological studies later today to see if there is any residual swelling or scarring," Dr. Goldstein started. "If that all looks good, we can check her out likely tomorrow. There will be a strict regimen with regard to what she can and can't do for a few days, but as far as we can tell, she's going to be absolutely fine."

Dr. Goldstein stood quietly while his news sank in. "Why don't you two go back to the hotel and get some rest? Come back later this afternoon and maybe you'll have a nice visit with Dana!"

"Because you never know where life is going to take you, and you can't change where you've been ... But I can! I really can!" Dana sat up abruptly. "That was a song I heard in my dream. But it's not true. I can change where I've been. I'm going to change where I've been." She was trying to pull off the covers, but the IV tube caught on the blanket and ripped out of her arm. The sensors that were attached to her head flew off and the buzzers screamed.

The charge nurse and the entire ICU staff came tripping to her bedside to calm her down. "Mrs. Gordon, you need to calm down. Shhhh! Calm down." Doris had been through this many times in the ICU. Often medications that patients were taking would cause very vivid dreams. "Mrs. Gordon, Dana ... wake up. Everything is fine."

"I am awake. I'm fine." Dana began to sit back and saw the tubing dangling by the bedside. "Oh, man. I'm sorry." The tape remained on her arm, but she could see the blood seeping from behind. It didn't look too serious so she laid back into the pillows carefully, and let the nurses fuss around her. Dazed, she fell back to sleep.

Doris cleaned Dana's arm carefully, and inserted a new IV needle, replaced the tubing, and adjusted the sensors. Dana was in a deep sleep again, but all of the nurses agreed the doctor should be consulted and maybe a change in her medication was necessary. She went out to the front desk, glancing around the waiting area and the private lounge, but Andy and Dana's mother were not there. She paged the doctor, and asked him to come up and check on Dana. Before she could hang up the phone, the screaming started again.

"Andy! Andy! I'm going to be the best that I can be. I choose to be the best that I can be." Dana gasped for breath. *"Andy please, don't leave me. I have the opportunity to fix this."* Dana was writhing around under the covers this time, making no attempt to get up, but living through something that was very real in her mind.

Doris ran into the ICU. "Dana, it's okay. You're safe. Andy isn't going anywhere. He loves you and will be with you." Doris knew Dana wasn't hearing her. She stroked Dana's arm, and then switched to her forehead. "Shhhhhhh."

"Mom?" Dana felt that familiar, calming stroke across her forehead. It always made her feel safe and secure when her mother would do that to her when she was sick or scared. *"Mommy? Are you there?"*

Dana's eyes remained closed, her body slumping back down into a relaxed slumber. Doris sat with her until the doctor arrived. He had just been through there an hour ago on morning rounds, and everything was fine. He had planned on discharging her tomorrow. "I think she's just dreaming," started Doris. "She yanked everything out and was trying to get up, but all her vitals have settled back down and she's in a pretty deep sleep now. "At first I thought it was some kind of psychotic break, but she was almost singing her words. Maybe it's an old song she knows. I don't know. You're the doctor."

"Doris, you know I have a tin ear. I wouldn't have even noticed it if she was singing! I'm not too concerned, though. Her heart rate is fine, respiration is fine." He stepped away from the bedside. "Haven't you ever had a dream that is so intense that it wakes you up and then you don't really remember what it was about the next morning?" He made a short note in her chart and looked up. "My family even asks me to mouth the words when we all sing happy birthday to someone." I'll be back at evening rounds and we'll see how she is doing then. I'll be here at the hospital most of the day, anyway, so if you need me, beep me."

Doris relaxed her shoulders. "Thanks for coming up so fast, doc. Ya know, I've been in the ICU many years, but there's something about this case. These two kids ... Somethin' special. I guess sometimes I worry more than other times about certain patients."

Marge stood at the side of Dana's bed just watching her. She didn't notice how much, if any, time had passed. She felt her pulse in her wrists and her neck as she silently stood, waiting. Dana had never really given her an ounce of trouble growing up. It was her two sons who were constantly getting into scrapes and accidents. What her own mother had told her had proven to be true. "Boys are harder to raise physically, and girls are harder, emotionally." Marge heard her own voice quietly repeating the words, when she was interrupted.

"Where's Dad?" Dana looked directly at her mother, fully knowing the answer. Marge was surprised, yet squirmed uncomfortably, looking for the right words.

"He couldn't make the trip," she started. "There's apparently a huge shoot this weekend. In fact, you were the one who scheduled it." Marge was sorry she said that. She didn't want Dana to be upset about anything, and especially about work, and she didn't want her to start turning things around and blaming herself. "But everyone knew you would be away on your honeymoon anyway." She tried to make it better; afraid Dana would react as she always does, with anger and venom toward her father.

"That's okay, Mom. Dad needs to do what he needs to do." Dana was almost surprised by her own words. It was almost as if someone else's words were coming out of her mouth. "I know he has difficulty being around sick people. He does the best that he can do. It's really okay."

Marge was flummoxed. "Who is this girl?" she thought. This was always the kind of situation where Dana would launch into a litany of reasons as to why her father was a lousy parent and why he was the cause of so many of her personal issues. "You must have really bumped your head hard!"

"No, I just have learned that people have to do what they have to do. I'm not responsible for his actions. Only how I react to it … and I can't afford to get upset right now." Dana lay in the bed peacefully, her heart monitor beating slowly and steadily, her blood pressure steady and low. "I want to get better and get out of the hospital, and that means letting go of anything that distresses me, especially something I can't change." Even Dana was baffled by her own serene composure.

Andy stood next to the bed on the other side, frozen. He looked down at his wife and then up at his mother-in-law. There was an eerie kind of silence penetrating the room, until the quiet was broken by the sound of a monitor buzzing two cubicles down from them.

Nurses and aides came running into the ICU. "Need you to clear out," whispered Doris as she breezed by. "Wait outside for a few minutes. Dr. Goldstein is on his way up anyway."

Andy and Marge did as instructed, and Dana shimmied down under the covers. The sounds of the ICU made her feel strange and disconnected, like she wasn't really there, somehow. She wanted to get up and go with her husband and her mother, but she knew that wasn't happening, at least not now. She closed her eyes as tightly as she could, trying to draw on whatever it was she had been dreaming about before, but she couldn't seem to remember what it was. She lay still, waiting for the emergency to pass, repeating to herself the phrase, 'this too shall pass, this too shall pass.'

In the waiting room, there was a peaceful stillness between Marge and Andy. They both remained lost in thought, trying to process their most recent conversation with Dana. What had she been dreaming about? How did her feelings about her father change so drastically? Is she still suffering from side effects of the concussion? Or the coma? Is it the drugs? Andy tried to make eye contact with Marge but she looked away each time. She wasn't ready to talk.

Dr. Goldstein zipped past them and bolted into the ICU directly to the patient whose buzzer was now quiet. Marge and Andy watched through the window until Doris abruptly closed the curtains. "That doesn't look promising." Andy turned on his heels. "Wanna go get a cup of coffee? This might take a while."

"I could use something stronger than coffee." Marge was still in a state of shock, trying to figure out the change in Dana. "But it is only 8:30 in the morning. Let's go down to the cafeteria." Marge looked back over her shoulder to confirm that the curtains remained closed and that nobody was emerging from the ICU. She grabbed her purse from the chair. "C'mon, my treat."

As Andy opened the door to the ICU waiting area, his eyes came upon Doris sitting at the charge nurse's desk, face in hands, softly weeping. His heart jumped from his chest to his throat. He wanted his mind to convince him that Dana was fine, and that Doris was weeping over another patient or maybe something personal. Marge, on the other hand, burst past him and without stopping to think, blurted out, "What's the matter? What happened?"

Doris looked up solemnly. "We lost the other patient." That's all she said. She gently placed her face back in her hands, mumbled what sounded like a prayer, and jumped up. "Back to work."

Marge stood there. She didn't speak. She didn't move. All she could do was go to prayer in her own head … and thank G-d that Dana was okay. She glanced upward for moment, took a deep breath, and then looked at Andy and said, softly, "I guess her number was up."

Andy was confused. How could Marge be so casual about death? Here this woman had been fighting for her life, just like Dana, and she just lost her battle, and all Marge could say was 'her number was up?' "That's a little harsh, isn't it, Marge?"

"I'm a fatalist. What can I say?" Marge was unfaltering. "I've been on this earth long enough to know that ours is not to question why …" She was interrupted by Dr. Goldstein.

"Marge, Andy, I have to tell you …" He was removing latex gloves from his hands and reaching around to untie his mask and robe as he spoke. "I had to leave surgery to run up here, sorry." He motioned them over to the corner of the waiting room. "Dana is doing great. I'd like to keep her here one more day. I'm going to move her to a private room later today, but you can plan on taking her home tomorrow."

"Home, home? Or can we finish our honeymoon," asked Andy excitedly.

"Honeymoon, by all means!" Dr. Goldstein sat on the edge of one of the chairs, rolling up his gown and mask. "In fact, I'd rather she be local for a few more days before she gets on an airplane. What was your itinerary?"

"We were only supposed to be here in San Francisco for another day or so. We have a bus tour booked to leave Thursday that goes down to L.A., and then we are supposed to fly back to Atlanta on Sunday." Andy was feeling a sense of disappointment. He knew Dana was going to be a lot more fragile and a lot of the things he had planned would have to be abandoned.

"Okay, here's how it will have to go." Dr. Goldstein was very serious. "Tomorrow is what, Tuesday? I'll discharge her in the morning. Let me see her in my office Wednesday afternoon to do another neuro check. It's right here at the hospital." His demeanor relaxed. "No sex for a few days. Can you deal with that?"

"Oh my God, of course!" Andy was just so grateful she was alive.

"If everything checks out Wednesday, I don't see why you can't follow through with everything as planned. She should be able to fly by Sunday with no problem. Her tests this morning were perfect."

Dr. Goldstein stood up, stretching his upper body and distending his neck. "I need to get back downstairs." He grabbed his garb and headed toward the door.

Dr. Goldstein knew Andy had a burning question left unanswered, but likely was too embarrassed to ask in front of his mother-in-law. He stopped at the exit door, turned around, and casually mentioned to Andy, with a wink, "Saturday, in case you were wondering."

CHAPTER 14

"Honey calm down. Just let them in." Dana admonished her husband for his driving as they pulled away from the hospital, as she always had. Andy was a safe driver, but certainly an impatient one. He had rented the car since they had to stay in and around the San Francisco area for a few days, and not knowing the final tab on the medical expenses, he thought this would save money. "We'll get there soon enough."

"Damn California drivers. It's like being in Atlanta at rush hour." Andy was actually relieved to be behind the wheel with his wife at his side. For a few days there, he wasn't too sure this was even going to happen. Patience was not part of his usual demeanor. He leaned on the horn. "It doesn't get any greener."

"Andy. Stop." Dana was calm. "We're not on a schedule. Let's just relax and take it easy." Dana turned around and addressed Marge who was staring out the window. "Mom, are you okay?"

"I'm fine. I'm just not sure I'm ready to leave you here yet." Marge wasn't the hovering kind of mother. She had always allowed Dana to make her own mistakes, learn from them, and grow. But this was different. She felt this deep in her gut. She had almost lost her baby, and was hesitant to let go again. It had been hard enough when she left home for college, and then when she married. That was only four days ago, but it seems like a lifetime.

"My flight is not for another five hours. Maybe we can do a quick sightseeing stop. I've never been out here, and the only thing I've seen is the hospital, the hotel, and a quick drive near the Golden Gate Bridge."

"Andy, can we go down to Fisherman's Wharf for lunch? Will that give us enough time to get to the airport?" Dana asked in a telling manner.

Andy recognized her tone. Now that was his wife. "Do I have a choice?"

"Well we're not going back to the financial district, if that's what you were thinking." Dana winked. She had no desire to see the Transamerica building or any of the other Insurance companies or any of the other money things. She pulled the wrinkled map out of her purse and began to navigate. "Turn right up here at this light."

Andy stopped short and leaned on the horn again. "Damn it. I keep forgetting there's no turn on red out here."

Within minutes, they were parked in a public lot and walking along Fisherman's Wharf. "Let's go to Alioto's. They have the best Dungeness crab and we can eat outside by the bay." Dana was almost dancing in circles, walking backwards. Suddenly, she bounced forward, losing her balance, was able to maintain her feet. Spinning around, she spotted the mime, hands on hips, with a pained expression on his face.

"Can't you people watch what's going on around you?" Andy was incensed.

"It was my fault, I'm sorry. I wasn't looking where I was going," Dana offered. The mime just stood there, frozen. Dana assumed it was part of his act but felt obligated anyway. "Andy, throw a buck in his tip jar."

"I will not. Jerk nearly took you out."

"Andy, come on. Lighten up." Dana reached into her purse, rummaging around at the bottom and found a loose dollar bill, and slipped into the mime's hand. "Have a beautiful day!" She grabbed Andy by the arm. "What's going on with you? Everything is fine. I'm fine."

Andy was still frowning. He gets this sour look on his face when he's not happy, Dana thought. And there's no consoling him once that's in place. She never likes the way he looks when he's like this. Not handsome. Not sexy. It's the ugly part of him. "Let it go. Are you going to let him live in your head rent free for the rest of the afternoon?" She didn't know where that came from. She only knew she wasn't going to let little things bother her anymore. Life is to be lived and enjoyed.

"Guess not." Andy let a small glimmer of a smile descend upon his face. "Let me go on ahead and see if they can seat us quickly, or at least get on the list." There he goes again, on a mission. This is something he will always do, Dana thought.

Marge and Dana took hands and slowly strolled along the wharf. The restaurant wasn't that far away, but they did have time to window shop and talk. "Mom, please tell Daddy it's okay that he didn't come. I'm okay with it."

"You're amazing." Marge still couldn't get over this change in her daughter. Dana always blamed Ben for everything that was wrong with her life. "He loves you, you know."

"I know." Dana chose her words carefully, because she didn't want to upset her mother the way she usually does. "Everyone has a history that makes them who they are. I can't expect him to be who I want him to be." Dana squeezed her mother's hand. "Having expectations of him that he can't meet will only make me resent him. I don't want to do that anymore."

Who put that in her head, Dana pondered. She continued. "I accept him for who he is, and know that he does the best he can. He's my Daddy and I love him."

Marge started to tear up. "Oh Dana, that's about the most beautiful thing you've ever said about him." She stopped and looked at her daughter … her adult, married daughter, who seemed to have a wealth of wisdom, serenity and peacefulness about her that wasn't there a week ago. Could being married just a week have done that? It had to be something else. Was it a brush with death? Perhaps. All Marge knew was that she is more proud of her beautiful daughter than ever.

"Here it is. Do you see Andy?"

"He's right inside waving us in." Marge took Dana's arm and pulled her close. "Let me just hold you for a second before we go in."

"Mom, stop. You're embarrassing me. Someone will think we're lesbians or something." Dana laughed to herself. Yeah, and so what if they do? There's nothing wrong with that. This is San Francisco, after all. Her love for Andy trumps any of her past experiences, even if Andy is weirded out by homosexuality. Maybe someday she'll tell him about her experience, maybe she won't. She isn't attracted to anyone but him.

"C'mon girls, let's eat."

"Well, now, that's the first pleasure trip we've taken since the ride to the Mark," Andy snickered as he pulled away from the departure drop off at the San Francisco International Airport. "I'm just joking, Dana. You know I love your mom." The levity disappeared in an instant as Andy slammed his hand on the horn. "Damn it all to hell anyway."

"You know, the speed limit around here is only 15 miles an hour," Dana calmly mentioned. Why is he so uptight, she wondered? Maybe he was afraid something else would happen? Maybe he didn't want to be away from the doctors just yet. I'm fine, she thought. "Why don't we just go back to the hotel and relax for a couple of hours, figure out what we can do for the day tomorrow, and then find a nice place for dinner. We just have to be at the hospital at 4:30 to see Dr. Goldstein. Otherwise, we're on our own."

"I think that's what worries me. Are you sure you're feeling okay?" Andy glanced over at Dana who was watching the road. It amazed her how the hills in San Francisco were so profoundly different than at home.

"I'm great! Think we could drive over to Lombard Street before we go back to the hotel? I've only ever seen it in the movies."

"Don't you think we should go let you get some rest? You only got out of the hospital this morning." He was worried.

"Nothing's going to happen. I feel great. We're only going a little bit out of the way." Dana already had an idea what was going to happen if they went back to the hotel. He would cajole her into resting, and then he would fall asleep watching television. Wait. No. Maybe not. He's usually pretty attentive.

Why was she thinking that way? "Come on; let's be even a little adventurous ... We only live once. Who knows when we'll get back to San Francisco? And we leave for LA on Thursday."

Andy put his blinker on and merged into traffic, and settled in to drive over to Lombard Street. She's right, he thought. It's right here in front of us. We need to get in and much as we can, as long as she's feeling okay. Why not?!

"Oh how cool!" Dana gazed upon Lombard Street from the bottom looking up. She couldn't get over the gardens and the hairpin turns and began to think better about having Andy drive down. "Okay, now I've seen it. Let's go back to the hotel."

"That's it? We came all the way over here and you don't even want to drive down? Andy was confused.

"Nope!" Dana would never tell Andy she doesn't trust him to drive down. "I'm getting kind of tired, and if we're going to go out later, maybe we better go back and rest."

"You're the boss."

"Don't you ever forget that," Dana laughed. She knew she would be able to have her way with Andy for the rest of her life. Love really is blind, she thought. He only wants me to be happy. Or as his father would put it, happy and quiet, mostly quiet!

Back at the hotel, they both wearily climbed into bed and snuggled into each other's arms. It seemed to Andy like an eternity since he had felt the warmth of Dana's body pressed close to him. It renewed that sense of security and comfort that was stolen from him in the elevator at the Mark Hopkins Hotel. He nestled his face in the crook of her neck and whispered, "I love you so."

Andy had been overwhelmed with so many different emotions in the last three days, he hadn't realized the toll that this experience had taken on him, and if he did, he never would have admitted it, at least not to Dana and certainly not to her mother. Within minutes, Dana's breathing had settled into a steady, slow purring, signaling slumber. It was only then that he let down his own shoulders and sunk down into the bed.

Andy's eyes began to water and he felt emotion erupting from within. Tears began to run down his face, his nose was running and he was starting to gulp instead of breathe steadily. He wriggled his arms out of the embrace of his wife carefully, and slid backwards in the bed to escape without waking her. Having successfully disengaged himself, Andy slipped into the bathroom and quietly closed the door. Leaning against the cool marble wall, he put his hands over his face and cried quietly.

When he turned around and noticed his reflection in the mirror, he was startled at how he had been reduced to blubbering child.

'She can't see me like this,' he thought. He's a man. He's her rock. He has to always be strong. Andy washed his face and took a few deep breaths. When he poked his head out of the door, he saw that Dana was sound asleep.

Andy silently found a comfortable spot on the couch in the suite, and began flipping through some of the tourist brochures. I'm going to plan the best day she's ever had, he thought. Tomorrow marks the beginning of our life together, or at least our second chance at it. He paused, looked up at the ceiling, and whispered, "Thank God."

Dana only slept for an hour, but that was just enough time for Andy to put together some ideas. She rolled over in the bed to see him scribbling out some notes on a scrap of paper.

"What are you up to?"

"Tell me what you think. Here are some ideas for our last day here in San Francisco." He proceeded to rattle off a full itinerary, starting with the very activity they were supposed to do the night of the earthquake.

"Let's start out tonight with the San Francisco by night tour and have dinner in Chinatown. And tomorrow, we can go to Alcatraz. There's a ferry at 9:00."

Andy had barely taken a breath. "We can come back and have lunch at Ghirardelli Square, and in the afternoon, after we see Dr. Goldstein, maybe we'll have time to visit the Coit Tower."

"Whoa slow down." Dana pushed back plush covers and wriggled around to a sitting position. "I think you might be a little ambitious there, honey."

Andy looked puzzled. Dana had never questioned his planning before. She always let him plan the vacations. Besides, he didn't want to waste any time while they were all the way out in California. Who knew when they'd get there again? She's the one who said it.

"I think some of this depends on how I feel. Some of it depends on what the doctor says, and I'll be damned if I'm getting into an elevator in some tower … What was it you said? Coit Tower?"

Wow! Andy had never heard Dana stand up for herself like this.

Cool, he thought. It's about time.

"You know, you're right," replied Andy. "Let's take each activity, one at a time, see how you feel, and see what Dr. Goldstein says tomorrow." He paused, focused on his wife. "Are you up for the tour tonight or do you want me to bring dinner in?"

"We can do the tour."

"Good. We have to be at the pick-up location at 6:30."

Dana glanced at the clock on the nightstand. "I'm going to jump in the shower." She threw the blanket all the way off the bed and if he wasn't imagining it, Andy would have thought she was skipping into the bathroom.

"Isn't it beautiful?" Dana asked.

"What?"

"The bridge, it's all lit up!" Dana tussled with her camera but wasn't able to get a good angle from the bus. After a minute or so, she gave up trying.

"I was looking out the other side." Andy pointed across the aisle of the bus out the window on the other side. "Look at that!" The bus was approaching Chinatown. "I'm hungry."

"Can I shop a little on this stop? Will we have time?" Dana was never a big shopper. She just wanted to pick up another little memento of some kind. Originally, she was collecting matchbooks, but since she got out of the hospital, she hasn't really been smoking too much, and hasn't even thought to pick up matches at the few places they've been since.

"I guess so." Andy just wanted to eat. He wasn't a big fan of Chinese food, but everyone back home told him that San Francisco's Chinatown had the best.

"Ladies and gentlemen, the tour will resume in approximately two hours. There are several restaurants in and around this area. Feel free to dine at the ones advertised on your tour brochure. A 10% discount is offered if you show them your tour ticket stub. We will be leaving at exactly 9:30, so don't be late. Enjoy your evening in Chinatown."

"Crap, I thought we were supposed to get a tour of the area." Andy sounded almost angry.

"Look over there." Dana pointed to a street sign on the corner that had the same picture on it as the tour brochure. "Maybe we're supposed to meet there."

Other bus passengers gravitated in that direction so they followed, and within three minutes, a small, Asian woman in traditional Chinese robes, carrying a bull-horn that was almost bigger than her, arrived at the sign.

"That's better." Andy was content.

"See," Dana was sounding condescending. "No need to get all upset. Just be a little more patient, Andy. We'll enjoy life a lot more if we're not always in a hurry."

"Uh … um, okay."

Dana walked directly behind the guide, drinking in everything she could. Andy remained a few steps behind, watching his wife, who he thought would find this whole experience 'lame' and would be nagging him for something to eat by now. What's gotten into her, he thought? He likes it, but it's definitely different. After a thirty minute walking tour, the group ended up in front of two of the three restaurants listed in the brochure.

"Pick one!" Dana proclaimed.

"After you, my dear." Andy opened the door of the nearest establishment, and the two dined on authentic Chinese cuisine.

The ride back to the hotel was filled with more information from yet a different tour guide. Dana could barely keep her eyes open, so Andy took notes on what she missed. When they arrived in front of the hotel, he gently woke her and let her up to the room.

"Long day tomorrow, honey. Why don't you get ready and climb into bed. I'll have room service send up a night cap."

"No thanks, Andy. I really don't feel like having a drink." Dana stopped and looked at her husband. "Did I say that?"

"Yup. That's okay, I don't really want one either."

The two retired to the overstuffed bed in the honeymoon suite, and spooning, fell off to sleep.

"Would you care for a Mimosa or a Bloody Mary with your breakfast?" Andy was trying to make sure Dana had everything she would want.

"No thanks, just orange juice, and maybe an English muffin." Dana put on the last bit of what little make-up she wore, spun around, and danced out of the bathroom. "What time do we have to leave to catch the ferry?"

"We have about an hour." Andy hung up the phone. "My turn. I'm going to take a quick shower. Breakfast should be here in about 15 minutes."

"Little seasick, are we?" Dana rubbed Andy's back. His complexion had turned from pink to that same hospital green as soon as the ferry left the dock, on its way out to Alcatraz.

"Only for you would I do this. I hate boats."

"I have a Dramamine with me, do you want it?"

"Makes me dizzy. I'll be okay"

The morning passed quickly with Dana, once again, drinking in everything she possibly could. Andy was more reserved, trying to overcome his bout with motion sickness, and not looking forward to the return trip to the mainland.

"Can you imagine this place fifty years ago?" Dana almost ran down the dingy hallway, trying to keep up with the tour guide. "And so many notorious criminals actually walked these same halls. Or escaped from here into the bay …"

Her voice trailed off in thought. For some reason she stopped walking, overtaken by a sudden chill. I could easily end up in jail, she thought. No, why would I? I'm a law-biding person … a teacher's pet … I don't break rules or do anything illegal. Or do I?

"Hey, what's going on in that head of yours?" Andy caught up to her.

"Nothing. Just day dreaming about this place." Back in the moment, Dana took Andy's hand, squeezed it, and pulled him along as she tried to catch up with the group. "What time do we get back?"

"It's almost over, except for the obligatory gift shop, if there is one here."

When they reached Fisherman's Wharf, they were a little rushed for time. They had to eat and get to Dr. Goldstein's hospital office in less than ninety minutes.

"Andy, don't order drinks again. We really don't have time to relax for this meal. You can do it at dinner, okay?

They left the car at the wharf and were able to take a cable car that left them only two blocks from Dr. Goldstein's office.

"Everything looks great, Dana. How are you feeling overall?" Dr. Goldstein slapped the file closed, after having done a few of those neurological tests that Dana found silly. She rolled her hands, she touched her nose, and she walked along a straight line. She was fine.

"Generally? Or Specifically?" Dana really didn't feel like herself but couldn't put her finger on what was causing the uneasiness, or whatever it was.

"Talk to me." Dr. Goldstein put the folder on his desk, crossed his arms and tilted his neck down, peering out over his tortoise shell glasses.

"I feel fine physically. No headache, no dizziness … Nothing." She hesitated. "I just feel different. I don't even know why." Pensive, she continued. "My mother and Andy, I think, even notice it. They are both kind of looking at me funny and reacting weird to some of the things I've been saying and doing." She paused again.

"Thing is, I feel very natural, and very much normal with it." "Sounds like a horrible disease." Dr. Goldstein smirked.

"You know, there was a time when I would have taken you very seriously, and panicked over that comment." They both laughed it off.

"Call me and let me know how the honeymoon went and how you're doing when you get home. I'd like you to check in with a neurologist when you get back to Atlanta. I have two or three names I can give you."

Dr. Goldstein got up from the edge of his desk and walked around to his chair, sat down and rifled through his Rolodex. As he was jotting down the names and phone numbers he spoke. "You had a good scare, Dana, but that's all. There is nothing to indicate any future problems from this incident, but just to be on the safe side, have someone keep an eye on you for a little while when you get back."

Dr. Goldstein stood, and walked around to Dana, handed her the paper and put his arms out for a hug. "Have a beautiful trip and a wonderful life together with Andy."

I intend to. God only gave me one life. I'm going to make the best of it, Dana thought to herself. One day at a time.

CHAPTER 15

"Again, you're up at the crack of dawn?" Dana put the pillow over her head. *This guy has way too much energy at six in the morning.*

"We have to board the tour bus by nine and I wanted to be sure you had enough time to shower, pack, and have a leisurely breakfast." Andy opened the hotel room door, and sure enough, a continental breakfast was waiting for them.

"Right on time." He leaned over and picked it up. "Don't get up.

I want to treat you to breakfast in bed."

Dana rolled over, puffed up the pillows behind her and prepared to be pampered. It was a strange sensation. She almost felt as if their roles were reversed. "What is this?" She sputtered as she took a sip of what she thought was orange juice.

"I asked them to send up a screwdriver for you." Andy was getting ready for a shower. "Why, don't you want it?"

"Not really. I don't think I want to be drinking today … not before we get on the bus, anyway."

"I'll have it." He took the glass from her, and then called room service to send up some plain orange juice. Andy called the desk and in two minutes, a bellhop was at the door. He pointed to the two large suitcases.

"That's all. We're boarding the tour bus right out front in about twenty minutes." He grabbed the tote bag from the bed, the camera from the desk, and the arm of his bride and they were off.

Boarding took less time then Andy had anticipated. Dana was busy glancing around the group. "There's nobody else here that doesn't have grey hair ... Where did you hear about this tour?" She wasn't too worried, because she had a way of getting along with everyone. She was only concerned that the sarcastic side of Andy would rear its' ugly head.

"Your dad's friend Danny ... You know the know-it-all travel agent. The one who booked the whole trip, having us leaving the hotel in Atlanta at 5:30 in the morning. That guy."

And there is was. Already. "Andy, relax. We'll have fun anyway." Just as the words tumbled over her lips, she heard a very polite, 'excuse me.' She turned around to see a young couple, likely another newlywed couple, standing before her.

"We were so relieved when we spotted you. Are you on this Parlour Car Tour down to Los Angeles?" Amy asked hopefully.

"Yep. I'm Dana, and that's Andy."

My husband Brian is over there. I'm Amy. Where are you from?" "We're from Atlanta, you?"

"He's originally from Minnesota, and I'm from Florida. We just got married."

"I kind of figured. I have one of those partly wilted corsages myself somewhere ..." Dana smiled. "Congratulations."

Relieved that the conversation wasn't going to all be about doctors and bowel movements, Andy plopped down on the seat next to Dana and fiddled with the camera. "If you're going to sit by the window, you have to be the photographer."

He no sooner got the words out when the bus driver came over the speaker with the instructions that at every stop, they would be rotating seats, moving up a row so that everyone got an equal chance to be on the Pacific side of the bus for some of those magnificent panoramic views to which we would be treated.

"Andy ..." Dana was hesitant. "Oh never, mind, you only live once."

"What honey?" Andy was concerned. Maybe she wasn't feeling well. Maybe her head was bothering her.

"Nothing. For a split second, for some reason I felt like I didn't want to sit by the window. But I'll get much better pictures that way."

Dana felt fine, physically, but there was something gnawing at her. I'm not afraid of heights, am I? No, of course not.

"Andy?" she asked softly. "I'm not a fearful person, am I?" Andy laughed out loud. "Really?"

"Yes, really."

"I'm beginning to think I don't know the answer. If you had asked me a week ago, I would have bet the farm that you wouldn't sit by the window, but now ... I have no idea what to expect."

Dana smiled. "The secret, my dear, is not to have any expectations at all. That way, you don't get disappointed."

Andy closed his eyes as the bus pulled away from the curb.

Dana snapped shot after shot of the city of San Francisco behind her, while Andy settled in for a nap. The bus driver had said it would be about two hours before their first stop in Monterrey. A Steinbeck fan, she was looking forward to seeing Cannery Row, although she knew it was nothing but a quaint little shopping area now. Her capacity to daydream about faraway places and romantic scenarios seemed to be resurfacing. The camera settled in her lap and she rested her head against Andy's which as now leaning against her arm. For the first time in a few days, Dana felt hopeful that everything was going to be beautiful.

The murmur of the other passengers coupled with the soft sound of the light wind across the window lulled her to sleep, and Dana drifted off into thoughts that seemed vaguely familiar. She felt groggy and dizzy. Is that real? Or am I dreaming? She tried to talk, but no words would come out. She felt the steady beating of her heart slowly speeding up.

Dana sat forward with a start. Glancing around, it took a moment to get her bearings. Andy was snoring softly, still on her shoulder. The busload of silver-haired tourists had quieted down. The view was still magnificent. Dana took a deep breath, realizing that at that moment, she was fine. Everything was just as it was supposed to be. She wasn't hurt. She wasn't drunk. It was just a dream.

"Ladies and Gentlemen," came the voice of the tour bus driver over a crackling speaker. "We will be pulling into Carmel in just a few minutes. We have made arrangements for lunch at a local restaurant, as well as giving you some time to sight see and shop."

Dana gently lifted her shoulder to wake Andy. "You hungry?" He grunted and groaned, but snuggled down closer. "Andy, wake up. We're stopping in Carmel in a few minutes." Andy slowly sat up, his glasses awkwardly dropping into Dana's lap, bouncing off the camera and dropping to her feet.

"I'm hungry." Andy leaned over and swiped at Dana's feet for his glasses."

"Well now isn't that a coincidence. We're stopping for lunch just for you!" Dana winked at Andy. He gave her a smirk … the smirk that made her fall in love with him.

"After our stop here in Carmel by the Sea, we will be shifting seats on the bus. Everyone must gather their belongings and move up one seat. Those in the last row on the left, please move to the right side. Those up here in the front right will move to the left side behind me." The bus driver was explaining, once again, the seat shift so that everyone gets an outside view of the Pacific Coast Highway at some point during the tour.

The bus slowed down as is seemed to shimmy off to the right onto a side street. It didn't look to Dana like it was a resort town. She sat back and waited. Andy, however, seemed to be agitated. "Where the hell is he taking us? I thought Carmel be the Sea was supposed to be right on the water."

"Relax, Andy. No need to get worked up or panicked. I'm sure he knows where he's going."

Andy looked at Dana in disbelief. Wasn't it her that usually flew off into panic when things didn't go as expected? Hmmm, he thought to himself. This is better. He sat back and looked out the window. The bus continued down a narrow tree lined, two-laned road that looked more like it was the back hills of Kentucky.

A few minutes passed and the tour bus emerged out onto a major thoroughfare with beaches on the left, quaint hotels, shops and restaurants on the right. Pulling off onto San Carlo Street, the bus came to a stop next to the Hog's Breath Inn. Before the driver could shift into park, most of the passengers were standing in the aisle pushing their way to get off. Dana sat calmly.

"Come on." Andy didn't have room to stand completely up as the overhang of the bus didn't allow it. We'll never get off at this rate."

"I'd rather sit and wait and let everyone else push their way. There's no hurry. We have plenty of time." Dana seemed very much at peace. "I'm much more comfortable sitting and waiting for the same five minutes."

Again, Andy looked at his Type A personality wife who seemed to be observing life rather than living it. "Are you okay?"

"I am fantastic. I just don't think we need to get all riled up in a rush." Dana didn't even believe her own words. She was always the one to unbuckle her seatbelt and be in the overhead while the plane was still taxiing; she was always the one who ran across a parking lot if she thought someone else was going to the same restaurant, to be sure she got her name in before them; it was Dana that always had to have the first appointment of the day with the doctor so she wouldn't have to wait.

"Okay, whatever you say. Just want my bride to be happy." Andy sat back down, took Dana's hand and squeezed it. "Love you, baby." When the last of the seniors filtered out, Andy and Dana made their way off the bus, deciding to eat right there at the Hog's Breath Inn.

"Do you have any "newly-weds specials?" Andy asked when the server came to the table. Dana's face turned red with embarrassment. She really did despise the fact that Andy was always looking for deals. She wondered if he would ever get past being so tight with his money. What was he so afraid of? Honeymoons shouldn't be cheapened.

"Congratulations! The best I can do is buying you a half carafe of our house wine. Would you like red, white or rose?"

"Honey, Which one?" Andy wasn't much of a wine drinker, but it was free. Dana could have whatever she preferred.

"I really don't care for any, thanks. Andy, have whatever you want."

"Huh? You don't want wine with lunch?" Andy was baffled. Dana never turned down a drink, and here they were in beautiful Carmel-by-the-Sea on their honeymoon. "Are you sure you're okay?"

"Yeah." Again, Dana was surprised too. "I just feel like I don't want to miss anything. I don't want to feel foggy, and you know me, I'll drink the whole thing."

The waiter stood there patiently. "Okay then, are you ready to order?"

Dana and Andy ate quickly and quietly, both contemplating the peculiar sense that something was different about Dana. Nothing was wrong, just different. In fact, they both seemed to feel that whatever it was, it was good. It was balanced; it was composed; it was sensible.

After lunch, Dana and Andy strolled the streets of Carmel, hand-in-hand, stopping in a few shops, but mostly enjoying the view of the water and the beaches, and people watching. They had only fifteen minutes left to board the bus and found themselves too far away from the Hog's Breath Inn.

"We better run!" Andy looked pained.

"We'll make it." Dana picked up her pace. "No stops along the way, but we'll make it."

They walked at a clip back along the streets and made it back to the bus in time. In fact, the other young couple had not returned yet either, so they were not even reprimanded by the bus driver, who seemed to be irritated. "This guy is in need of an attitude adjustment," said Dana. "Can't let it bother me. I'm not responsible for his words and actions ... only my own, and my reactions to him." She shook her head as if to jar something loose. Dana wondered where that came from. I'm supposed to give him some snide remark back, she thought. Hmm, oh well. This is much nicer.

When everyone was boarded in their new seats, the bus driver announced that they would be travelling back north a short way, with a brief stop for a photo op of the Pebble Beach seals before settling at the hotel for the night.

"They're really cute." Dana reached back blindly toward Andy for the camera.

"I think they're kind of goofy looking. Why are you taking so many pictures of them?" Andy wasn't quite used to Dana's love of photography yet. He only had the cash register going in his head of the cost of processing all of these rolls of film of pictures the damn seals. "Really, Dana, stop."

"What's the matter?"

"It costs a lot of money to process that film. You've taken enough pictures of seals."

Dana stopped. She doesn't know why, but Andy is really tight about some things. I guess this is one of those things that isn't worth battling over, she thought, so she put the lens cap on the camera, climbed back up the small incline and hugged him.

"It is so magnificent out here," she said under her breath. "Only God could paint a picture like this."

Back on the bus, Andy and Dana were now in the second row on the right side of the bus, heading toward the hotel.

"Do you want to go exploring tonight or do you want to eat right at the hotel?" Andy knew what he wanted her answer to be. Dana knew what Andy wanted her to say.

"Let's stay in."

"Again, nothing to drink with dinner?" Andy was again, puzzled. "For some reason, I just don't want to drink anymore. It's like I think I'm going to miss something if I do." Dana was really okay with this. It was Andy that was so concerned. "There's no law that says I have to drink, is there?"

"No, but do you, mind if I have one?" "Not at all! Enjoy!"

Dana ordered a light supper. She had picked up some sweets at a cute little bakery in Carmel that she had intended to have for a late night dessert in the room. The only thing missing was the whipped cream.

Andy ordered a large steak, practically raw. Dana never understood how he could eat it when it was hardly cooked, but that was how he liked it, so she left it alone. After dinner she sent him to the desk to see if there was a grocery store or convenience store nearby to get the whipped cream, while she went back to the room.

Andy kicked at the door gently with his toe. "Dana my hands are full. Open up."

Dana flitted across the room to the door, her lace-trimmed satin robe floating behind her. This is the first chance she has had to wear this bridal set. It was a day earlier than the doctor had said it was okay for them to do this but she didn't want to wait anymore.

She slowly opened the door, revealing only her head, and with tongue in cheek she asked, "Who is it?"

Andy looked irritated. "Come on, open up. This stuff is awkward." "You were supposed to get some whipped cream. Why so awkward?"

"They had a sale on sweatshirts that say Pebble Beach. Thought they would make good gifts for everyone when we get back. Open the door."

Dana swung the door open to reveal her peignoir and grabbed one of the bags. "Did you buy another suitcase too? How are we going to pack these?"

"Wow. Who cares?" Andy dropped everything, including the whipped cream, and kicked the door closed behind him and was all over Dana.

"Hold on." Dana picked up the whipped cream and put it in the tiny refrigerator. She turned around for a split second and then thought better of it. "Forget the dessert." She grabbed the package back out of the refrigerator and handed it to Andy. "I can be your dessert tonight."

By the time she had the plastic lid open, Andy was sprawled across the bed, sporting an erection and motioning her to join him. Dana slipped her robe off her shoulders and let it trail off to the floor behind her as she climbed up on top of him. She placed the whip cream on the bed next to his head and leaned down, kissing him, gently at first.

Andy tried to pull her closer, but Dana resisted. "Slow down, my sweet. We have plenty of time." She leaned over again, this time open mouthed, thrusting her tongue into his mouth, exploring every inch of it. Andy responded by holding her close, grabbing her buttocks and thrusting his pelvis upward. She could feel his penis pressing against her, unsuccessfully penetrating her nightgown, so she sat up and pulled the gown up over her head, tossing it to the floor.

When Dana leaned forward the third time, Andy buried his face between her breasts. She captured him between her legs and they held each other for what seemed like a lifetime.

When they awoke, the whipped cream was gone, the dessert was still in the refrigerator, and Dana and Andy lay naked, entwined with each other and the sheets.

"I love you forever." "That's hokey."

"It may be hokey but it's true." Dana threw the covers off and headed toward v "Where do we go today?"

"We go down through Big Sur and we stop at the Hearst Castle.

We stay in Pismo Beach, or San Luis Obispo."

"Never heard of it." Dana was climbing into the shower. "What time do we have to be ready to leave?"

"We have about two hours to shower, pack, and eat breakfast." Andy was still lying in bed, amused that he was fully aroused at the thought of Dana in the shower. He got up and called in to her. "Can I join you?"

"I'm almost done, but sure." Dana had gotten used to that question. She used to hate it when Andy invaded her shower time. It seemed that was the only time she had to unwind. This time, though, she waited in anticipation and when he climbed in, she threw her arms around him, and wiggled, sharing her soapy body with his.

"Do we have time for this?" Andy asked hopefully.

"The way I see it, we don't have time to not." Dana's attitude about showing Andy how she feels about him was the most important thing she could do.

"Now I know that knock in the head did something to you. But I like it, I like it." Andy turned Dana around and bent her down by the waist. He mounted her from behind.

Andy and Dana eagerly boarded the bus for the next leg of the trip. She had loaded the camera with the fourth roll of film, and that was only since they left San Francisco yesterday.

"Can you lay off some of the less interesting pictures today?" Andy had finished stowing the carry-on bag overhead and plopped down into the seat next to Dana. "Believe it or not, you haven't seen the best parts yet. Wait to we get back out onto the Pacific Coast Highway down through Big Sur. Your jaw will drop."

CHAPTER 16

"Sir, you need to come down from there." The bus driver was less than cordial as he yelled up to Andy. "Sir, we are boarding to leave."

Andy had climbed out a rocky protrusion on the west side of the highway, having told Dana it was like the last peak at Charlie's Bunyan in Smokey Mountain National Park. He wanted to get a few pictures of the Pacific, so he had climbed up the incline to the top and inched his way out to the edge.

Dana was less pleased than the bus driver. She was already having enough trouble getting used to the drop off over the side of the road in Big Sur. The rotation of seating on the tour bus left her and Andy in the front right of the bus, and Andy had cajoled her to sit by the window because she was so much better with the camera than he was. There was no way in hell she was going to climb on the rocks knowing that there was at least a football field drop down the side. I'll be happy when we get to San Simeon, she thought.

"Andy, come on."

Andy snapped one more shot with Dana's camera, and then slung it around his neck. He had to turn around and get down on his hands and knees to shimmy back the three or so feet to get a foothold on the rocky crag he still had to climb down.

"It's okay," Dana reassured the bus driver, who was now pacing back and forth. All of the other passengers were on the bus waiting for them. "He's an Eagle Scout. He knows how to do this."

Just as her words tumbled out, Andy lost his footing. He tried to grab a small branch protruding from the rock to interrupt his fall, but his arm got tangled in the camera strap, which hooked on the branch instead. "Crap!"

Andy stumbled to his left, smacking his shoulder and then his head on the granite that now made up most of Big Sur. He rolled down into a pile of brush at the bottom. His fall had only been eight feet, but it had been enough to knock him out.

As he went down, he had been thinking to himself, this must be how Dana felt in that elevator. after all we've been through, now this?

"Andy, wake up." Dana was angry. "We're going to be late for this marriage counselor and this was your idea in the first place."

Andy couldn't rouse himself. He felt like he was melted into the ground. It was a familiar feeling, like he had too much to drink. He had an empty feeling, too …

He heard Dana, but he just couldn't wake up. After some of the things that happened last night, he wasn't sure he even wanted to …

www.ingramcontent.com/pod-product-compliance
Lightning Source LLC
Chambersburg PA
CBHW031457120626
46545CB00005B/1648